CANDIDATE FOR A MIRACLE

Wisdom from the Miracles of Yeshua

JEANNE METCALF

1st Edition 2014
2nd Edition 2023

Cegullah Publishing & Apologetics Academy
International Copyright © 2023
www.cegullahpublishing.ca

All rights reserved.

ISBN # Textbook: 978-1-926489-88-9
ISBN # Workbook: 978-1-926489-87-2

Cover photo © iStock # 1359927727 (2023)
Cover design by Jeanne Metcalf.

COPYRIGHT MATTERS

This book is an original manuscript by the author, protected by international copyright laws of Canada. Therefore, none of this author's work may be reproduced, in part or in whole, or stored in a retrieval system, or transmitted in any form or by any means, electronic, mechanical, photocopied, recorded or otherwise for commercial use without the *prior written* permission of the author. However, it is possible to receive permission to use short quotations for personal use, or use in a group study, or for permission to copy certain passages, or to make portions of the writings available for overhead viewing. Simply, contact the author[1] to request it.

SCRIPTURE MATTERS

All scripture quotes originate from KJV[2], public domain. However, the name of God appears as YeHoVaH, not LORD. See appendix for more information.

---

[1] To contact author, see *Contact Page in Appendix*
[2] KJV King James Version. This version, when written, referred to all humankind as "mankind". When reading this version, unless the passage itself refers to a particular person, to which the text specifically refers, apply the message to all humankind, regardless of gender.

DEDICATION

I dedicate this book, first, to Yeshua Ha' Maschiach, (the Saviour) Who came to save, heal, and deliver[3].

Then, to all those who walk in Master Yeshua's footsteps experiencing God's miraculous best for their lives and in turn, help others to receive the same.

---

[3] *"The Spirit of the Lord GOD is upon me; because YeHoVaH hath anointed me* **to preach good tidings unto the meek; he hath sent me to bind up the brokenhearted, to proclaim liberty to the captives, and the opening of the prison to them that are bound; to proclaim the acceptable year of YeHoVaH,** *and the day of vengeance of our God; to comfort all that mourn; to appoint unto them that mourn in Zion, to give unto them beauty for ashes, the oil of joy for mourning, the garment of praise for the spirit of heaviness; that they might be called trees of righteousness, the planting of YeHoVaH, that he might be glorified."*

Isaiah 61:1-3

COURSE 304
SECTION 1: REACHING FOR THE MIRACLE

CHAPTER	TITLE	PAGE
	Introduction	9
1.	Recognize God's Authority	15
2.	Recognize God's Integrity	29
3.	Recognize God's Perception	45
4.	Recognize God's Resources	61

SECTION 2: RECEIVING THE MIRACLE

5.	Recognize God's Willingness	81
	Water Turned into Wine	
6.	Recognize God's Sovereignty	109
	A Large Catch of Fish	

COURSE 305

	Candidate for a Miracle (Continued) t	
7.	Recognize God's Presence	129
	Stormy Sea Calmed	
8.	Recognize God's Faithfulness	155
	Feeding of the 5000	
9.	Recognize God's Awareness	169
	Money in the Fish's Mouth	
10.	Recognize God's Dominion	179
	Fig Tree Withers	
11.	Recognize God's Supremacy	197
	Walking Upon the Water	
12.	Recognize God's Empowerment	209
	2nd Catch of Fish	
	Conclusion	219

APPENDIX

About Jeanne Metcalf……..…………………………..	251
About CP & AA…………………………………..	253
About the King James Version…………………….	237
A Name to Honour…………………………….…	231
Contact CP& AA………………………………..…	254
Miracle Subdivision Index…………………………	247
Other Books by this Author………………………..	249
Salvation's Message…………….............................	238
Scripture Index…….…………………………….....	244
Sinner's Prayer & Lifetime Commitment……….....	242

CANDIDATE FOR A MIRACLE

COURSE 304

SECTION 1

REACHING FOR THE MIRACLE

GROUNDWORK
for the miracle
with needed mindset shifts.

In reaching for your miracle

Introduction

"Is any thing too hard for YeHoVaH? At the time appointed I will return unto thee, according to the time of life, and Sarah shall have a son".

Genesis 18:14

Anyone, at any time, in any place, under any circumstances, whatsoever, can receive a miracle. All one need do is recognize the potential of their situation as a platform for a miracle. Then, reaching out to the only One Who can do all things, they become a candidate for a miracle.

This book entitled "Candidate for a Miracle" invites readers to come along as, together, we investigate the miracles of Yeshua. Each miracle under study displays God's power in some very difficult situations facing individuals in the time of Yeshua. Additionally, each miracle demonstrates one aspect of the supernatural, a topic today which calls many to investigate.

Investigating the supernatural makes room, then, to invite the same to manifest in our life.

Now, to receive a supernatural answer to our need, to receive our miracle, two major components come to mind: *God and us*. God's role, the Bible reveals. It shows us His Heart, which reinforces His desire to respond to our need.

Additionally, the Bible teaches how to align with God so we can receive from His miracle power. Therefore, miracles, themselves, carry a strong link with the Bible and its teachings. Thus, it makes sense, to look at the miracles in the Bible, analyze them, learn from them, and then, apply it to our lives.

When thinking of miracles in the Bible, many ponder about Yeshua's many miracles as recorded in the gospels. These miracles, thirty-seven in number, fall into three basic categories:

- Power over nature
- Power over sickness, disease, infirmities and the like
- Power over death and darkness

Each miracle, as the Bible relates it, conveys facts about the situation, the people involved, as well as how the miracle occurred. These events, which more than summarize God's amazing abilities, convey God's compassion for humankind, as well as His desire to walk with His human creation through any trouble that touches their life. We can learn much, as we approach a study about the miracles of Yeshua.

To *quickly* assess the miracles performed by Yeshua, leaves a person without adequate information on how to apply things to their own life, and also does Yeshua a great *injustice*. On the other hand, a deeper, meditative approach produces an enjoyable palette of spiritual food for the believer, as well as give a pattern for one to follow.

Thus, an in-depth approach to the miracles of Yeshua seems most appropriate. To take this approach with all thirty-seven miracles, however, produces a tremendous size book, therefore, in this book, we present only eight miracles of Yeshua, each one exhibiting God's power over nature.

Before investigating those eight miracles, however, we lay down some needed groundwork. This means, we look at some groundwork the future recipient of the miracle needs before they receive it. Simply put, this means highlighting some specifics to help the miracle candidate align with any biblical requirements to receive their miracle, e.g., mindsets that produce a confidence in God as they look to Him for their miracle.

Then, as we examine the eight miracles within this textbook, we look at actual candidates, their miracles and how these took place. Keeping in mind our goal to obtain wisdom from the miracles of Yeshua, "Candidate for a Miracle" presents the facts of the miracle in the following manner:

- **Background Setting:**
  This shows the history of the problem, along with the main characters involved in the miracle story.

- **Operative Mindsets:**
  This aspect exposes the way individuals think, *prior* to the miracle, often uncovering attitudes required to change.

- **Miracle Platform:**
  This identifies the situation, which may not always be easily recognized. For example, Yeshua's invitation to feed the 5,000 stunned the disciples as their minds immediately assessed their food supply as inadequate.

- **Revelation of God:**
  This aspect shows a candidate's necessity to draw near to God to know more about the One to Whom they believe and trust to help them.

- **Miracle Specifics:**
  This reveals the particulars of the miracle, identifying the supernatural need.

- **A Surface Meaning:**
  This exposes the immediate result of the miracle as well as the immediate significance of it.

- **A Deeper Meaning:**
  This reveals deeper spiritual realities, so they become embedded in the recipient's mind, soul, and spirit, thus giving them a well from which to draw to receive their miracle.

- **Mindsets Challenged:**
  This points out how miracle recipients learned to think differently, ways they might adjust their thinking to receive in their own situation. Additionally, it opens a door for onlookers to examine how their approach aligns with the needed mindsets to receive their miracle.

When finished examining these eight miracles in this manner, readers should discover how to present their life before God, positioning themselves in the best manner to receive their miracle in the needed areas of life!

In other words, "Candidate for a Miracle, presents an invitation to readers to study and learn how to position themselves to receive from God the miraculous intervention needed for their life.

So, dear reader, use this book and its references to biblical precepts, to learn and grow in your concept of miracles. Step into the days of Yeshua, and let the Holy Spirit guide you as, together, we examine eight of Yeshua's amazing miracles, each one verifying heaven's stamp of approval on the Saviour, the Living Son of God.

Discover or *refresh yourself* on some important and amazing attributes about God. Such information helps to appreciate God's care of His creation, boosts a person's faith, and helps to align mindsets to enable receiving from God.

Dear one, as you read this book, (and/or use the accompanying workbook[4]) deepen your understanding of the God, Who loves you more than you could even imagine! Embracing that love, recognize your personal platform for a miracle. Then, discover that you are, *like many others before, around, and after you, a*

Candidate for A Miracle!

---

[4] To use the accompanying workbook, helps to take a closer look at scripture passages, to study them and gain a better understanding. This also helps to build faith! Look for the accompanying workbook by ISBN # 978-1-926489-87-2.

1

In reaching for your miracle
Recognize God's Authority

"For ever, O LORD, thy word is settled in heaven".
Psalm 119:89

Yeshua's miracles, so many in number, powerfully indicator God's heart to all who seek Him. Each miracle stemmed from Yeshua's relationship with His Father and shows us much about their intimate relationship. After all, Yeshua did nothing without His Father, and thus, His relationship with His Father sheds light on knowing God.

What did the relationship between Yeshua and His Father look like? As I ponder that topic, I recognize a pure and holy *two-way connection*, that delighted *both* the heart of the Father and that of the Son. Flowing out of that connection came the revelation of the Father, so mankind can behold the proper reality of Him. Surely,

Yeshua, even in the manifestation of the miracles recorded in the Bible, presented to us, forever, a solid, dependable knowledge of the amazing characteristics of the Father's heart towards mankind. Knowing that heart, helps to receive from Him!

Through Yeshua's behaviour, in all situations conveyed in the Word of God, we see communicated to us the exact image of the Father. As Yeshua demonstrated this, we know how the Father reacts in any given situation. Then, we can embrace and embed deep into our being, the Father's response. Thus, through Yeshua's expression of miracles, clearly, we hear God's timeless message that He is alive, and interested in humankind's well-being. Constantly, He bends His ear to the many needs of humankind, whether those needs be great or small.

From a quick read of the Bible's recorded miracles, we immediately know that no matter the reason for seeking God's help, God desires to respond positively to those who call upon Him. Yeshua showed this to us, presenting evidence in the miracles performed that, definitely, God desires, *yes wills*, to bring solutions in our lives that meet our needs, even if it means *the performance of a miracle*.

WHAT IS A MIRACLE?

A miracle is God's response to an impossible set of circumstances, which mankind cannot resolve. It is mankind's supernatural answer from God. In fact, in thinking about miracles, to realize things stand out:

1. Miracles, before manifesting, require *endurance* through some very disagreeable circumstances, which often seem overwhelming, undesirable, and generally incredibly stressful. These, however unwanted, nevertheless, create the need for the miracle.
2. Miracles, once realized, bring a positive ending to those extenuating and impossible circumstances, which gave us *the platform* for the miracle.

That platform, no matter its dreadful details, once recognized, causes a focus on a solution. With eyes focused on the only One that reigns above all circumstances, the candidate for the miracle cries for help. Those cries arises to God's ears. When spurred on by faith, the situation shifts, *preparing the platform to expect its solution to come! In other words, it creates a stage* for God to enter.

In fact, the Lord looks for such situations to show Himself as God:

2 Chronicles 16:9 a)
"9 a) For the eyes of YeHoVaH run to and fro throughout the whole earth, to shew himself

strong in the behalf of them whose heart is perfect toward him[5]" ...

It is a sad reality, but a person never receives a miracle of provision, unless they experience lack. In that circumstance, God shows up as Yahweh Yir'eh, the Lord Who provides. [6] Likewise, a person who is ill never experiences Yahweh Rapheka[7], until He arrives on the scene and brings forth healing. A person simply cannot experience a miracle, of any kind, unless the situation warrants it. Every miracle, which answers the extreme circumstances of humankind, comes *only* into situations that require them.

YESHUA AND MIRACLES
As we look at the miracles of Yeshua, we see that His ministry on earth touched people whose lives were in extreme pain. He healed lepers, after the decay of their bodies had been underway by that dreadful disease. His anointed hands reached out to touch paralyzed bodies, those with eyes that could not see, or ears that could not hear, or mouths that could not speak. The list goes on and on of people in extreme circumstances,

---

[5] The quote is part of verse 9. The verse ends with this comment, *"Herein thou hast done foolishly: therefore, from henceforth thou shalt have wars"*. Unfortunately, the mankind to whom this word came failed to release his situation to God's Hand, and the end of that failure meant the King would continually have wars.
[6] That name actually means "the Lord, Who sees ahead".
[7] This name means "the Lord Who Heals".

yet, when reading about the accounts of their miracles, we simply must not overlook the events that preceded their miracles!

Sometimes, in reading accounts in the Bible, we forget that these people recorded in the Word, were just like you and me. Their clothing, most likely, looked different; their language was different also. Their lifestyle was very far removed from ours today; however, exactly like us, they were flesh and blood. Thus, they had real aches and pains; real doubts and fears; real disappointments and real broken hearts. Often, they suffered deep rejection as people looked upon them. Some, such as lepers, were exiled to a desolate place. Some, such as cripples, were forced to beg for a living. Some, such as epileptics, were stared at, mocked, and ridiculed as they experienced a seizure in a public place.

We must remember, when looking at their miracle, to consider their accompanying trauma, which made up the platform for their miracle. Why, might you ask? In seeking God for a miracle, for our own person or for another, if we, dear reader, overlook their trauma, their pain, and the effects of such on their humanity, we miss the tender heart of God, as He reached out and touched them. In other words, we miss a foundation for the extension of God's hand in any miracle: *His compassion and love for humankind.*

As we look at miracles, and as we see Yeshua's extended hand, we need to also remember that Yeshua walked the earth also as a real person. He understands the realities that we face daily. He knows the feeling of pain in His body, for He endured a crucifixion. He knows the humiliation of a public whipping, the condemnation of an innocent mankind, the jeering of crowds who saw Him as a rebel. He knows the distance sin places between God and mankind as He became sin on our behalf. That experience broke His heart! He is moved with compassion for us, no matter our circumstances.

Hearing of the many things Yeshua faced, as well as those whom His love touched, should help us to realize that the God of the Bible is a friend of mankind. He desires to touch the lives of anyone who calls upon His name. By faith, we know that none of the records within the gospels are fictitious, nor are the realities of the people who needed them. Each account of a miracle bears record to a situation causing distress, in one way or another. Each account shows the situation presented to God as a platform, upon which, God chose to show Himself as mighty.

As we recognize and identify with these things, we find common ground, not only with another person's problem, but also with the solution God provided. In that, we build our faith to see God's solution realized in our lives, right where we live, *for the day of miracles has not ended.* This is so because God never changes!

Knowing that about God makes His gift to us, in the pages of the Bible, an invaluable asset! It is always His current instructions to us since it contains His powerful Word. It will always burst over with doses of reality! This inspired Word of God can and must become a vital part of our life, a hands-on manual, to show us the best ways to resolve the many problems we face while upon this earth.

Recognizing the Bible as God's authoritative Word, always current, helps us to face our challenges, especially when looking at needed miracles. With Bible wisdom, we can make each difficulty in our life a platform for God's appearance, and at the same time, we position ourselves to become a candidate for a miracle. In taking the Bible's approach to life and the problems which must be resolved, we won't miss God's best for us and settle for less!

Yeshua came as a Saviour, a mighty One indeed. As we reach out for Him in that capacity and receive Him as such, we move towards the best possible breakthrough in our life. We move towards a solution and to the only One Who can walk us through every situation. Once we've embraced Yeshua as Saviour, however, we must remember that His salvation embraced more than forgiveness for our sin! The provided solution by God included salvation to the uttermost end!

Hebrews 7:25
> "25 Wherefore he is able also to save them to the uttermost that come unto God by him, seeing he ever liveth to make intercession for them."

"Saved to the uttermost" includes being redeemed by God, in every way possible! That means saved to the height, depth, breadth, width, and length of all matters that touch a person's life. Its effect reaches back to our very beginning of life, forgiving past wrongs and moves forward, taking us into eternity, forgiving everything along the way. In every instance, God's grace brings us mercy and His mighty power aligns us with the many benefits of being His child. David, the Psalmist put it this way:

Psalm 103:1-5
> "1 A Psalm of David. » Bless YeHoVaH, O my soul: and all that is within me, bless his holy name. 2 Bless YeHoVaH, O my soul, and forget not all his benefits: 3 Who forgiveth all thine iniquities; who healeth all thy diseases; 4 Who redeemeth thy life from destruction; who crowneth thee with lovingkindness and tender mercies; 5 Who satisfieth thy mouth with good things; so that thy youth is renewed like the eagle's."

In short, God's redemption, under the First Covenant, brought many benefits. Amongst those benefits are forgiveness of sins, healing from all diseases, as well as redemption from destruction, which means we have Eternal Life. God's plan for salvation crowns those in covenant with Him with His lovingkindness and tender mercies. We are satisfied with good things, so that our youth is renewed like the eagles. Keep in mind, that was promised under the First Covenant! How much more do we, as New Covenant believers, have ready and available benefits to touch our lives!

Simply put, no matter the event touching a life, God's power promises to bring to pass everything needed. Such an ability to meet those needs indeed constitutes a Mighty Saviour! In looking at the benefits too, we see a steady and constant flow of the Father's heart to His children. Once we know that heart, our connection to God grows in leaps and bounds.

Then, as we know the Lord as Saviour and learn to understand and walk in His Ways, we are ready to express that knowledge to others. We reach out to others in the same manner as Yeshua reached out to us, to show everyone we meet something about the endless love of God that we've experienced. We follow the guidance of the Holy Spirit, Who, of course, comes into the life of every believer, so that we might demonstrate the mighty works of God, or more accurately, the Holy Spirit demonstrates God's mighty miracles through believers, as they walk with Him.

John 14:12-13
> "12 Verily, verily, I say unto you, He that believeth on me, the works that I do shall he do also; and greater works than these shall he do, because I go unto my Father. 13 And whatsoever ye shall ask in my name, that will I do, that the Father may be glorified in the Son."

Thinking about the divine call of the Body of Messiah worldwide, to do the works of Yeshua, and even greater works because of His position with the Father, we realize its expression by following in the footsteps of the Master and His declaration:

Isaiah 61:1-2
> "1 The Spirit of the Lord GOD is upon me; because YeHoVaH hath anointed me to preach good tidings unto the meek; he hath sent me to bind up the brokenhearted, to proclaim liberty to the captives, and the opening of the prison to them that are bound; 2 To proclaim the acceptable year of YeHoVaH,"

Yes, the Holy Spirit comes upon each believer, anointing each one to preach good tidings[8] unto the

---

[8] This is the gospel message

meek, bind up the broken hearted, proclaim liberty to the captives, open prison doors to those that are bound, and proclaim the acceptable year of the Lord, which extends from the cross until Messiah's return.

Believers must follow in His footsteps and that means expressing the Father's heart towards all. Part of that heart is to realize, through the power of the Holy Spirit, miracles in the lives of those desperate for such. That heart, as far as I understand the Word of God, is to bring *life* into any situation touching their body, mind, soul, and spirit, to bring them into perfect liberty, so they may function in the way that God designed them to function.

God's Heart desires to see none held in the captive snare of the one who speaks destruction. These thoughts compare to what Yeshua said:

John 10:10
"10 The thief cometh not, but for to steal, and to kill, and to destroy I am come that they might have life, and that they might have it more abundantly."

So, dear reader, at this chapter's close, I pray you see yourself as a candidate for a miracle. I trust that you look at your circumstances or those of others in need as in a unique place to present their platform to God, (their stage) for His entrance. In doing so, remember:

1. God's authority over all things.
2. Yeshua's arms stretched out towards you as you draw near to Him.

As the pages of this book continue to unfold before you, I pray that as you examine the miracles of Yeshua, important aspects of His character leap off the pages. I hope you hear and receive the heartbeat of His great love, His expansive compassion and mercy towards all humankind, *including you*[9].

A PRAYER FOR YOU:

So now, as this chapter closes, I trust Yeshua to help you to receive all He has for you. May He teach you to open wide the door of your life in every avenue of your existence. May He reach you to recognize every platform in your life in these days, as well as days to come, so you can present them to Him to reveal His glory!

---

[9] Sometimes people recognize His love for others but fail to realize their life receives the same love! IF this is you, take a moment and thank God that He loves you, then, receive His love.

May your life experience a powerful visitation by the Holy Spirit, as Yeshua brings you near to Himself, to encourage, strengthen, and bless you. May He receive great honour through your life. May He show you to others as one who, *not only understands His miracles*, but knows *how to set the stage to receive them ... and of course ... prays for others to receive them, also.*

2

In reaching for your miracle
Recognize God's Integrity

"Declaring the end from the beginning, and from ancient times the things that are not yet done, saying, My counsel shall stand, and I will do all my pleasure:"

Isaiah 46:10

In the Body of Messiah[10] today, some forget, or perhaps never knew, that God, from a long time ago, decided how He would respond to the many issues regarding humankind's life upon the earth. One issue was a major decision which required His response to fallen mankind. God, through His foreknowledge, understood the day would come when sin would enter the world, and along with sin, death. He thus readied a plan of restoration. *On God's part,* the bottom line of that plan saw to a provision of a Saviour, as well as a means of presenting that Saviour

---

[10] The Body of Messiah is the overall collection of believers worldwide.

for mankind's recognition, and the bottom line, *on mankind's part,* was a method to recognize their sin and need for a Saviour, as well as how to avail of that provision.

On God's part, He sent and revealed His Only Son, Yeshua, as Saviour. Then, so humankind would recognize God's Saviour, He prophesied His coming. He did that through the Prophets, and what some might find surprising, He additionally prophesied it through the First Covenant *sacrificial system.* That system provided a detailed method to receive forgiveness of sins from God. Of course, the Torah, under the First Covenant, detailed the behaviour God required from His People. Once they honestly assessed their own behaviour, comparing it to what God required, they would recognize their failure (their sin). With prescribed methods to follow to receive forgiveness of sins, they could then present the proper sacrifice to God.

On the surface, as First Covenant saints followed closely the prescribed sacrifices, their faith in that provision of God gained for them what they needed: *a covering for their sin, and through their faith, salvation.* Beneath the surface, unknown to the believer, God's plan of Salvation lay hidden or enclosed in prophetic types or pictures. These the Bible calls "Shadows".

As First Covenant believers practiced their faith, they sought God, received forgiveness for their sins, *but they did so without a full revelation of God's plan*. God, however, when looking upon the First Covenant sacrifice presented to Him, saw everything that sacrificial system portrayed, or prophesied. Later, God revealed what He saw to humankind through Yeshua.

After the Death, Burial, and Resurrection of Yeshua, the Holy Spirit opened to believers the prophetic shadows formerly concealed within the First Covenant. Early, first century, New Covenant believers, and every believer since, receives forgiveness of their sins with a full knowledge of the revealed plan of Salvation. Yet, what we often forget to realize, is this: *God always saw that plan fulfilled and complete, even when it was depicted in a First Covenant sacrifice.*

"Why is it so important to think like God," you might ask? There are many good reasons why believers should learn to think like God; among them, to attain an understanding about how His Kingdom works. While the Bible says, "God's thoughts are higher than our thoughts"[11], the born-again believer has been given

---

[11] Isaiah 55:9 For as the heavens are higher than the earth, so are my ways higher than your ways, and my thoughts than your thoughts.

a wonderful open door to think like God. What is that open door?

> 1 Corinthians 2:16
> " 16 For who hath known the mind of the Lord, that he may instruct him? But we have the mind of Ha' Maschiach."

Due to that fact, God equipped believers with the mind of Messiah. We have an open door to think like Messiah thought, to speak like Messiah spoke, (the Word of God), to love like Messiah loved, to do the works of the Kingdom of God as Messiah did. All a believer needs to do is yield to Messiah's mind within. That happens as, from the written Word of God, we learn God's Ways, God's Wisdom, God's plans, and purposes and so many other wonderful things about our God.

Simply put, a believer shifts gears from his own thoughts and limitations, to soar by agreeing with God, His thoughts, and His infinite abilities. To think like God, we believe God's Word and apply it to our life and every circumstance touching it.

Looking back to the topic of salvation, most believers think about salvation as it occurred 2000 plus years ago, at the time when Yeshua hung on the cross. God, however, perceived that salvation *finished* at a different point in time.

> Revelation 13:8
> "13 And all that dwell upon the earth shall worship him, whose names are not written in the book of life of *the Lamb slain from the foundation of the world.*"

According to the above scripture, the Lamb of God, (Yeshua) was slain "from the foundation of the world". In order to think about that salvation and all its benefits, the way God perceives it, we simply shift our thinking. We embrace thoughts of our God, Who lives outside of time, and thus, for Him, Calvary happened, *not* as we see it today, *as a past event*, but rather as **an eternal existent and present event**.

God first planned mankind's redemption. Then, *in His Kingdom*, a kingdom without a time frame, He set it in place. At the point in our time, when He framed the world, salvation, **in God's eyes,** was already complete; hence the scripture, "the lamb slain from the foundation of the world". (Revelation 13:8)

Connecting *this to a timeframe*, the way we think, we could say that God established Salvation ready and waiting for the moment sin entered. Hence, He **predetermined,** *before sin entered* the world, how He would handle sin. He chose, way back before He set in place the earth's foundation, that He would forgive mankind through the shed blood of the Lamb of God, Yeshua.

With regards to understanding that salvation, the full revelation came through Yeshua. God determined from the beginning, long before the dawning of humanity upon the face of this earth, how to handle the fall of mankind and its consequences of sin and death.

Yes, God settled the matter on how mankind must receive forgiveness, and enter into a relationship with God, in the time of their existence upon the earth, as well as eternally afterward. Mankind's only requirement is to learn of God's plan, agree with it, and then accept it. Thus, mankind's volition in the process makes Salvation a very personal experience, accessible in every generation.

Once in God's Kingdom, believers, who live their life one day at a time, must shift again into a higher gear, thinking now in terms of eternity. This is necessary to understand God's plan of Salvation and all its benefits. Why? The answer rests in the fact that God sees everything as *already done, as finished.* Since it is complete, that means the topic is *not open for additions.*

Salvation, in God's eyes, along with every aspect God included in the "Salvation Package",[12] is perfectly complete. It needs nothing more added to it, nor will anything ever be taken away from it. In personal terms, each believer has, ready for their use, every benefit attained at the cross, given without partiality! Its package is unwrapped, and the contents received by "faith".

Keeping the thoughts of God's predetermined counsel in mind, believers recognize the things upon which God decided and implemented earlier, when the Lamb of God was slain. This speaks of God's great integrity. He decided to redeem mankind, and no matter how horrible humankind degraded, as long as humankind reached out for repentance, repentance came to them[13].

Even regarding the adversary of humankind, God decided how He would deal with Him, and in that decision, God will not change His mind. God decided to handle, on behalf of all humankind the one the world calls the devil, or what the original Hebrew

---

[12] This term is here presented to liken our benefits from the Lord to an employment package. The comparison stops, however, in the way benefits come. They are not earned benefits, but unmerited favour, free of cost to us.

[13] God destroyed humankind in the flood because flesh held only thoughts of violence. They looked not to God for repentance even though God's call for repentance echoed for many centuries/.

Scriptures calls "ha satan"[14], To perceive this subject in God's eyes, He judged the adversary, who Yeshua called, "the prince of the world", and then, through Yeshua's life, death and resurrection, God broke His power. We know this by the words of Yeshua.[15]

John 16:8-11

"8 And when he *(speaking of the Holy Spirit[16])* is come, he will reprove the world of sin, and of righteousness, and of judgment: 9 Of sin, because they believe not on me; 10 Of righteousness, because I go to my Father, and ye see me no more; **11 Of judgment, because the prince of this world is judged.**"

John 12:31

31 Now is the judgment of this world: now shall the prince of this world be cast out.

---

[14] In Hebrew, ha satan means the adversary, but KJV and other translations interpret that word as the devil, and capitalize it to indicate a proper noun, which denotes respect. Many Christians, knowing that, will not capitalize the name, and prefer to say, ha satan.

[15] John 16: 11 Of judgment, because the prince of this world is judged.

[16] Author inserted the brackets so the reader will understand the subject reference in the scripture.

That means, God made a definite judgment and strategic move against the "prince of this world", namely "ha satan". He judged him *(the prince of this world);* found him guilty in the courts of God; issued a perfect and just verdict. Then, acting on that verdict, He cast him out. This means that ha satan no longer **sits in the position as prince of this world.** He has been dethroned, removed from his place office.

This is good news for the believer in Messiah! Part of our "Salvation Package" includes victory over "ha satan" (the adversary and his schemes). By the power of the Holy Spirit, this is not only possible, but it is a reality! A true, born-again believer's life becomes **effectively different** after they, in faith, fully accept God's plan of Salvation[17], which includes a forsaking of sin, walking away from unrighteousness to pursue holiness.

God, in His infinite wisdom, made other decisions, too. Each decision was part of God's predetermined counsel and implemented a long time ago. For example, regarding humankind's health, God provided a solution for restoring it. In looking at the

---

[17] Many good books are written on this subject. Rev. Jeanne Metcalf has a few teachings that touch upon this topic, such as "Kingdom Keys for Kingdom Kids", which speaks of the victory given to the believer. It is available from "Forward ... March!" Ministries. (How to order the book is found on the last page of this book)

physical well-being of humankind, to understand God's plan of restoration, we must look at several things:

1. God made humankind whole, or complete, in the Garden. In other words, God made humankind healthy and that is how God desires humankind to live.
2. Sin and death entered the world, and from that time on, humankind's body experienced diseases, infirmities, and the like.
3. If one is to think like God, we must remember that the results of sin, with its consequence of death, *was never* God's perfect plan for humankind. Negative effects on the health of human beings and other created beings living upon the earth, came only from a decision of mankind to disobey God. With that choice to elevate mankind's will above God's, mankind's disobedience opened the door to disorder, chaos, destruction and the like, none of which were ever part of God's perfect order. To help us understand God's plan regarding the health of humankind, we must keep these facts in mind, not forgetting that any form of ill health was never part of God's perfect plan for humankind.
4. Thus, God's predetermined counsel for restoring health was also set in place when the Lamb of God was slain. We know this by reading a passage by the Prophet Isaiah:

Isaiah 53:

> "5 But he was wounded for our transgressions, he was bruised for our iniquities: the chastisement of our peace was upon him; and *with his stripes we are healed.*"[18]

When Yeshua walked the earth, *which, by the way, was during the dispensation of the First Covenant,* Matthew, the disciple of Yeshua and author of the book by his name, quoted this scripture as prophesied by Isaiah, seeing its fulfilment in Yeshua:

Matthew 8:16-17
> "16 When the even was come, they brought unto him many that were possessed with devils: and he cast out the spirits with his word, and healed all that were sick: 17 That it might be fulfilled which was spoken by Esaias the prophet, saying, *Himself took our infirmities, and bare our sicknesses.*"

In the first quote, Isaiah prophetically declared God's plan regarding transgressions and iniquities, as well as ill health, for he said, "with His stripes we are healed'. Later, in Matthew's time, when Yeshua walked the earth, the writer of that gospel saw Yeshua as the fulfilment of Isaiah 53, when he wrote, "That it might be fulfilled which was spoken by Esaias (Isaiah) the

---

[18] "with his stripes" refers to the blows of the whip upon Yeshua. (The italics and bold print inserted by the author.)

prophet, saying, *Himself took our infirmities, and bare our sicknesses.*

Still, that same passage in Isaiah appears, one more time, in scripture, but this time in the writings of Peter, the Apostle.

> 1 Peter 2:24
> 24 Who his own self bare our sins in his own body on the tree, that we, being dead to sins, should live unto righteousness: by whose stripes ye *were healed*".[19]

Peter, writing after the cross, recorded the activity of healing as *past tense,* thus showing that He understood healing was finished at the cross, *just like salvation.* This indicates that, once again, God made up His mind regarding healing for humankind. This is a very clear proof that Yeshua, indeed, was God's fulfilment of Isaiah, but it also means something personal for each believer: *God wants the human body healthy,* since He planned for that wellness as part of our "Salvation Package" set in place through Yeshua on the cross.

As one reads of the miracles in both Old and New Covenant, we see evidence of healing as God touched the spiritual, physical, mental, and emotional health of

---

[19] Italics added by the author.

humankind. This Lamb slain before the foundation of the world included provision for healing *in every way,* just as it included forgiveness of sins, no matter the offences, originating from humankind's behaviour.

All those healed, under the First Covenant, benefited from the Lamb of God prophesied and foreshadowed in that covenant, and all, since the cross, avail of the same one-time sacrifice of Yeshua, the Lamb of God. God desires each one receive the full benefits of their "Salvation Package", including their healing, any way it's needed.

No timeframe, not even the 2000 plus years since the cross, changes anything that God included in our "Salvation Package". God predetermined it and set it in place for all of time, and it rests on His ability to bring it to pass in the lives of individuals, in every generation under heaven! His consistency to keep His Word and make it applicable in each believer's life rests in the fact that God changes not!

Malachi 3:6
"6 For I am YeHoVaH, I change not;" [20]

---

[20] This is the first part of the verse. It continues with another thought; therefore, it was not included here. Feel free, however, to look up the remaining portion of the verse for yourself in the Bible.

Hebrews 13:8
"8 Yeshua Ha' Maschiach the same yesterday, and today, and for ever."

SUMMARY:

Recapping the thoughts thus far, God made up His mind, or predetermined how He would handle many important matters to do with the care and well-being of humankind upon the earth:

- He settled the sin question. When mankind asks, He will always extend forgiveness, no matter how horrible the sin or how often the offence. He never says "No" to forgiveness, when asked from a sincere, faith-filled heart! He simply cannot.
- When mankind asks for victory over ha satan and his plans for them, God again made up His mind as to how He will respond. He provides the way of escape, the way of victory. He cannot go back on His Word.
- When it comes to human beings living in good health, God already decided, a long time ago, His answer. It is a resounding "yes". He cannot change His mind and say "No!" One only needs to reach out to the Lord and ask, and then receive His prescription for healing.

In reaching out for your miracle, dear reader, recognize the integrity behind the One Who gave His Word!

Look at the many benefits that God included for you in your "Salvation Package". Know God honours them. Also, remember God gave you, and all believers, an amazing inheritance in Messiah. It waits for you to discover and appropriate.

"But as it is written, Eye hath not seen, nor ear heard, neither have entered into the heart of mankind, the things which God hath prepared for them that love him."[21]

---

[21] 1 Corinthians 2:9

In reaching for your miracle
Recognize God's Perception

"In my distress I called upon YeHoVaH and cried unto my God: he heard my voice out of his temple, and my cry came before him, even into his ears". Psalm 18:6

God desires a loving and close relationship with all His creation, especially with those He originally created in His image, namely humankind. His perception of that relationship, to keep us more in line with our original purpose, necessitates that we understand and obey His ways. This truth, perhaps untasteful to many, keeps us more in line with how He created us and why.

Unfortunately, the first creation, Adam, fell. Sin entered and immensely distorted the very image of God in us. Thus, when God links together in a relationship with us, He wants to restore us to our original state, however, we must agree with that goal and follow His guidelines for it to happen. To recognize that we shifted away from our initial creation state is imperative. We must learn, that in aligning with God, our choices must alter. Only aligning with God's will, or in other words, learning to do things God's way, do we enter into an awesome relationship with Him, one that brings fantastic communication, just as God designed it, originally.

In this chapter, looking at that restored relationship with God, remember, first, the wide-open door to connecting with Him. That open door is Yeshua[22]:

John 10:9

> "I am the door: by me if any mankind enter in, he shall be saved, and shall go in and out, and find pasture".

As we enter that door, (Yeshua), and begin our relationship with the Father, YeHoVaH, we begin our relationship with Him as we learn to share our heart with Him. In sharing this aspect of our life, we soon learn that God desires to respond or communicate with

---

[22] If you do not understand how to walk through the door of Yeshua to the Father, please read Salvation's Message in the Appendix.

us. After all, relationship[23] develop through communication and time spend one with the other.

In our relationship with the Heavenly Father, we must recognize that the Father wishes to respond or converse with us. He does that through the Holy Spirit. It may be through the written Word, through dreams, through visions, or an anointed messenger He sends to speak with us, however, once we walk through that open door, Yeshua, we have access to a two-way conversation with the Father and opportunity to develop a wonderful relationship with Him .

Not receiving from God, very often, lies within *humankind's perception of God*, and conclusions of what *they think* He is like. In grabbing hold of a relationship with God, as a rule of thumb, remember that God desires to communicate with the epitome of His creation, humankind. Realizing His will to connect and converse, to receive from God, whether it to understand His will or receive an answer to prayer, simply embrace the fact that God wants to communicate with "you" and expect Him to do so. Recognize "your" not exception to the rule, then move forward. In other words, dear reader, to receive from God in all avenues of your life , simply adjust your

---

[23] John 14:6 Yeshua saith unto him, I am the way, the truth, and the life: no mankind cometh unto the Father, but by me. (Once one is redeemed through Yeshua, they can then come directly to the Father.)

thinking. Like other believers before and after you, learn to think like God, and then, receive from Him.

When believers learn to think like God, they walk by faith. Thus, our approach to God changes from thinking what we love and how we think, to develop an open ear to what God loves and how He thinks. God's thoughts and His world embodies the realm of faith,. Learn to develop a *faith mentality, and you'll learn to think like God.*

Faith is the key ingredient when talking to receive anything from God, as the scriptures says:

Hebrews 11:6
6 But without faith it is impossible to please him: for he that cometh to God must believe that he is, and that he is a rewarder of them that diligently seek him.

When we ask God in faith that He will respond, we place ourselves in an expectancy mode.

As Hebrews 11:6 states, God desires that all approach Him holding to the fact that He exists, that He is alive, able, and ***willing*** to respond. Coming to Him in that manner, puts us in a place to watch for His rewards, for He does recompense the diligent seeker with the appropriate response to their need.

"Diligently seek" *(from Hebrews 11:6)* carries with it the idea of *actively seeking.* The Greek word interpreted as "diligently seeking", however, carries another aspect of seeking the English words do not convey. In the Greek language, the seeker has an attitude of expectancy, so their active seeking results in a realization of their goal.

In other words, the searcher searches, *expecting to find what he seeks*. Pertaining to God, which is the context of the verse, one seeks God, knowing He exists and they, thus, expect to find Him. When we seek God actively, we shift into an expectancy mode, waiting for Him to respond. God, Who easily recognizes and identifies the searching heart, responds. He willingly puts the required answer in the person's pathway, so they soon *discover God's reality* in a greater way. Once a person comes to God, **on His terms**, which includes a personal acceptance of His Salvation as He prescribes, the door stands wide open for a relationship with Him.

That relationship, which moves a person closer to God as they actively seek Him because they know He exits, puts the person into a category, known as a ***believer*** … you know … ***one who believes***! As such, when they pray, they know, ***by faith***, that God not only listens **to** their prayers, ***but He listens for their prayers to answer them.***

A STUMBLING PLACE TO AVOID:

Once redeemed, when believers approach God in prayer, many fall over a stumbling stone of *human thinking*. They perceive God as judging their prayers on the merit of their words, or persuasive ability. Nothing could be further from the truth! At the moment of salvation, God accepts the believer, who has a truly repented heart. Salvation has opened a wide door to communication with God! Believers need not worry about fancy words, for God sees the heart, and that heart speaks louder than the words, phrases and sentences put in plain or fancy order.

Other believers perceive God as partial, hearing and responding to another believer better than He'd hear and respond to them. Some reasons to think that might include an idea that another knows Him longer, or is doing more good works, or expresses themselves better, etc. These are *pitfalls* on mankind's thinking, not God's. To avoid them, we learn to think like scripture!

In accordance with scripture, God's response to believers is not based on any form of their own *personal merit*. God's inclusivity is seen in salvation's invitation and onwards:

John 3:15-16
15 That whosoever believeth in him should not perish but have eternal life. 16 For God so loved the world, that he gave his only begotten Son, that whosoever believeth in him should not perish, but have everlasting life.

"Whosoever" is the first word to note. That word includes everyone, meaning God excludes no one from salvation. As long as there is life in a human being, a living member of this earth, they fall into the category of "whosoever". Thus, any person, as long as they are alive, no matter what they have done, if they desire to forsake their sins and receive God's Salvation, the door is open. *Remember, we must learn to always think like God! When He has done a thing, such as Salvation, He can't say "no" when we ask to receive it on His terms, because He's already said "yes"!*

Recognizing that God's "whosoever" applies to all at salvation, let's move forward to look at the life of every individual believer. When it comes to the other benefits found in Salvation, again God says "yes" and not "no". We know this is so because, in God's mind, it is already done. This, Paul the Apostle knew when he wrote these words to the believing church in Corinth:

2 Corinthians 1:20
"20 For all the promises of God in him are yea, and in him Amen, unto the glory of God by us."

Thus, in receiving from God, we must learn to think *exactly like He thinks*! It is already done! We agree with God to receive His promises for our life or for that of others.

Moving into our everyday life, we find there are limitless opportunities for encounters with God, beginning in our prayer life and moving outward as we live. There is a world of adventure to explore in walking with God, sharing your world with Him, asking Him to help you walk above situations, beyond problems and in line with His will and with what He has already done for you.

For sure, as believers bring forward, from their hearts to His ears, their deepest desires, He listens intently to each one of His children. He delights and treasures each and every personal encounter of sharing. He loves it when His children value His Word and seek His will, His love, and His counsel. Liberally, He lavishes the answers, and in His Love, willingly He aligns the believer in a position to receive from Him. In other words, it is important that we understand God's perception of us. As we desire a relationship with Him, we must remember, He desires the same for He created us for relationship. His thoughts about a relationship with us is paramount in His thinking.

Speaking into that relationship, did you know that God desires for humankind to receive what we need, *far more than* we desire to receive it? So great is His love and compassion for us! On a personal note, dear reader, remember that *just as He completed your salvation,* **He completed your full access to all the** *provisions* that stem from the cross, **excluding** nothing. He did this for you because He wants you to receive it all! The door is open, dear one, simply walk through it!

So, from this point on, as you read through the following chapters, you'll read about what God did for others through the life of Yeshua. You will see how He responded to mankind's needs. As you read, say to yourself that, *just as God moved in that situation on behalf of another, He will move in my situation for me, too, because I am His child.* While God may not do **the exact same thing, as far as an identical solution**, He'll respond with love to your unique situation, to your personal needs. He will, without a doubt, bring about a ***suitable solution***, tailor made for that unique problem presented to Him from your life, in a way that you'll receive it.

Receiving His solution depends upon *your willingness* to bend to God's ways. Extract from your mind, however, any thought that says you are the exception, or you are the one God chose <u>not</u> to answer. Delayed answers often happen because people ***refuse to align*** with God's plan or answers in a situation.

The problem of receiving, dear reader, never lies with God. It always lies with humankind.

With these things in mind, let's look at the point of this book: *to help you receive* whatever you need from God, (call it a miracle), whether big or small.

> As you go through the many pages of this book, use each miracle event *as a lesson to help you think like God thinks.* His thoughts are far higher than ours and thus, outside the *box of human thinking, nevertheless, with scriptural training the thoughts and the mind of Messiah as given to believers active, thinking like God becomes doable!*

As you study the miracles in this book, (and others found in your Bible):
- let each situation, and the way God answered it, present a confidence that God *will answer* any need, where people depend upon Him, believing and trusting Him to do so.
- let faith arise in your heart, as you read.
- let each situation thrill your heart with God's powerful way of answering a need.
- Let yourself think of the situation in front of you as an open door, showing not just what God can do, but how much *He wants* to do something for you, too!
-

Consider the following example:

*A physician, when looking to build his practice, does not put out **ads for healthy people**. Doctors, of course, desire to keep healthy people well, but their main goal is to attend to people who are not well. Each unhealthy person that comes to a physician expects to receive a solution of some sort for their particular need. That solution might include a prescription or some other treatment to resolve the problem. If that sick person finds the doctor an integral part of resolving their problem, helping to restore them to good health, they are sure to tell others about that doctor.*

God is the Great Physician, as well as many other wonderful things. For those who have a need, a desire for healing in their body, they have many choices to make. One choice is to pray to the Great Physician and ask for His help. Now, once they have done so, they have taken that problem, that negative situation in their life, and positioned it for an answer from God. That need, therefore, has just become *a platform* for a miracle.

Through prayer, the believer elevates, into God's hands, a situation waiting for God to arrive and show Himself strong! That situation now has a wide-open door for God to enter. Yes, that situation awaits God's touch! When one thinks like God, they expect His arrival, in some manner or another, to resolve the situation.

Whenever you look at your situation, or that of another, remember not to look at the problem, no matter how desperate, as one that is unresolvable. God always has a solution! *If you look at circumstances as hopeless, you have just excluded God!* You accidentally missed your chance to turn the problem into a platform for a miracle!

Please don't ever, dear reader, look at any person or circumstances as doomed to failure. If ever tempted to do so, please resist the temptation. If you can, thank God for the situation, because it gives you an opportunity to see God work on your behalf. Please consider that situation an invitation for you to become a candidate for a miracle. *All you need to do is set it up like one!*

If, dear read, as you look at each situation you face as a *potential platform* to position an individual or a circumstance, as a candidate for a miracle, you have just discovered an open door for God to show Himself. This again is thinking like God, not mankind. It aligns with the words in the following scripture:

2 Chronicles 16:9
> 9 For the eyes of YeHoVaH run to and fro throughout the whole earth, to shew himself strong in the behalf of them whose heart is perfect toward him. Herein thou hast done foolishly: therefore, from henceforth thou shalt have wars.

In this unique situation, Asa, the King of Judah, had an extremely difficult situation, one that looked hopeless. Asa decided to resolve this situation on his own, you know, do it his own way. When he did that, he ignored the platform for a miracle, a place for God to show Himself as strong. Instead, he reached for mankind's help, looking to a powerful nation to save him. God was displeased with this King of Judah, who should have known better.

In God's eyes, Asa acted foolishly.

This is really a wonderful revelation of the heart of God, dear reader, and the situation stands as a lesson for all people, in all situations, whether simple or extreme. God actually *searches* for situations upon the earth, amongst His people.

No matter whether situations require simple solutions or complicated ways out, God is always ready to act. All one need do is extend an invitation to the Lord, asking Him to respond, and then, align in whatever ways might be necessary[24], and wait, expecting the miracle to manifest!

---

[24] As you read the miracles, note how people needed to align, in one way or another, with certain things, which they needed to do. For example, the mankind with the withered hand needed to stretch out his hand, which is impossible for mankind, yet the action, done in alignment with God's command, saw the miracle realized. You will learn more about these things later.

FURTHER CONSIDERATIONS

Perhaps you have not thought of God in the way this book outlines thus far. If not, consider shifting gears! Change your thinking to agree with the way the Bible teaches us to think, which is "to think like God". When you do, you will see that the God of Abraham, Isaac and Jacob, the God of Yeshua, is a very powerful God, with endless resources. How awesome, too, that He looks for situations to show Himself strong. He understands that people, through various circumstances, invariably end up in hard places.

So, should you, or a loved one or friend, find yourself in one of those hard, difficult, or even impossible places, remember to perceive things the way God perceives them, Knowing God's Ways through studying His Word, helps you to do just that!

Know, too, that God does not stand back, enjoying your pain and suffering. He longs for an invitation to come along side of you, comfort you and resolve the situation! However, remember that God requires an invitation to do so, first. He respects your personal space, and that of others, too. So, invite Him to come along side and be your answer! As you wait for His Hand to manifest in that matter, invite God to help you know His ways, also and then, agree with the ways of God He showed you. That makes the situation much easier to resolve.

As you read of people within the New Covenant structure, you might consider this check list:

- Identify their extreme circumstances, looking at their need and how they invited God to help them.
- Note how God brought answers to their requests.
- Look at what they did until the answer arrived.
- Watch for places where participants in the miracle changed their thinking to receive their miracle.
- Always examine God's response *through Yeshua*, and remember, as He responded through Yeshua, to bring an answer to the problem, He also responds today.

When it is your turn to position a life for a miracle, set the platform for that miracle by giving it to God as a place to show Himself strong. Put your faith in place with your prayer fully confident that, due to Yeshua, God hears you, identifies with your situation and also has a planned solution waiting and ready for release. By faith, accept that solution, thanking Him for it[25]. Expect to *realign your thinking (and perhaps your actions also), wherever necessary*, and speak to God

---

[25] You probably will not know the details of how God will resolve this situation, but just thank Him that, no matter what it takes from His end of it, He will supply.

about your willingness to do so. In this way, you set yourself up to expect a miracle!

> Remember, dear reader, that every situation in your life, or that of another's, *even ones that look absolutely hopeless,* stand before you as a potential platform for a miracle *if you choose to make it such.*

All one need do is invite God to bring to pass ***His perfect will*** in the situation. From that moment on, let your faith arise to a new level of expectancy from God, for you have set the scene for yourself, or another, to become:

"A candidate for a Miracle!'

In reaching for your miracle
Recognize God's Resources

In the Bible's earliest pages, we see that the God of the Bible is far greater than all things that He created, including the world in which mankind lives. Therefore, ***His resources surpass our wildest dreams!*** For example, in the opening pages of Genesis, God, as Creator, displays His magnificent artistic hand in the formation of the heavens, the earth and all that is in them. His resources used: His Word, "let there be …."

Turning a few pages further, we see the compassion of God and the tender care He provides for mankind after the fall. In His great mercy, we see a promised Redeemer to restore all humankind back into fellowship with their creator. Vast indeed lay the resources of forgiveness and the plan that God laid out for human beings to spend an eternity with Him.

Moving past those opening chapters in Genesis (the book of beginnings), we arrive at the place where the Almighty One calls an idol worshipper named Abram to forsake all and follow Him. In obedience, Abram leaves his former life and all he knew, to follow God and travel into a land that God would give him. As time progresses in the relationship between God and Abram, God solemnizes a covenant, at which point he gives Abram a new name: *Abraham*. This name means the father of nations, and what is quite ironic, Abraham, at that time, had no child, no heir from his body in which to leave a legacy.

In the more senior years of Abraham, at age 100, God keeps His promise to Abraham. At this stage in Abraham's life, when his body and that of his wife, Sarah, are far past childbearing years, as good as dead. Their resources to see God's promised fulfilled lies only in their hope of God as their earthly resources miserably failed to produce a solution. On the other hand, God shows up with His infinite resources alive within His presence, and He rejuvenates the aging bodies of both Abraham and Saran. As a result, from the loins of Abraham and the womb of Sarah, God brings forth a miracle child. Abraham, age 100 and Sarah, age 90, become the proud parents of a son they name Isaac. As time moves on, history proves that nations sprang forth from Abraham, just as God promised.

Moving into Exodus, we see the children of Abraham, known as the Israelites, suffering beneath the hand of a cruel tyrant known as Pharaoh. Through God's Divine intervention and power, the Israelites, *(estimated by some to be as many as 2 million)*, exited their place of slavery. By the power and might of Almighty God, they left their former life in Egypt to walk with God in a land of Promise.

Leaving Egypt was not easy. However, through a series of events, Pharaoh finally agrees to let God's people go, then, later reneges on his decision. Pharaoh sends troops to destroy the escaping slaves. This situation culminates at a point where the Israelites stand before a body of water, which blocks their way of escape in front of them. Behind them is Pharaoh's army consisting of weaponry and determination enough to destroy every Israelite.

By a mighty hand of God using some of His powerful resources, the body of water (the Red Sea) once blocking the way forward, opens wide, providing a way of escape through the middle of the sea! The Israelites cross over on dry ground, with a wall of water standing on either side of them.

They reach the other side and then they see the army of Pharaoh racing after them, following their same way of escape. Protecting His children from certain death, one more time, God acts. The walls of water relax, returning to their normal state, completely drowning the enemy. By these mighty acts, God forever released the children of Israel from the bondage of a cruel and wicked taskmaster. That exodus, orchestrated and executed by God, released Abraham's children to follow their pathway to freedom, to possess the land promised to Abraham.

In the book of Joshua, the Israelites move into their Promised Land. Here, the All-Powerful God of Israel goes out with the armies of Israel, causing cities to fall before them. In Judges, we see God's mercy reaching down to the very disobedient children of Israel in order to set them free from their oppressors. Time after time, God executed mighty deliverances for them.

Next, in the books of Samuel and Kings, we see the beloved of God, King David, arise to power, beginning with an incredible victory as a young mankind, and moving into his life as a grown mankind. Through this king's obedience and love, God stretches the borders of Israel to reach to the limits promised to Abraham.

Following King David, in the reign of his son, Solomon, we see Israel embracing false gods, and consequently losing unity within their own nation, and eventually losing ground within their kingdom borders. Assyria moves into the Northern part of Israel, dispersing the tribes from that region. Babylon invaded the south, eventually capturing Jerusalem and taking captive all those living in Judah. Babylon left its mark on the face of the land, even burning to the ground the magnificent temple erected to honour the God of Israel.

Yet, even with all the physical evidence which pointed to an impossible restoration of this nation, the God of Abraham, Isaac, and Jacob shows Himself as mighty. By His Hand moving through King Cyrus of Persia, God calls for a restoration of the descendants of Abraham to move into Jerusalem, to rebuild the temple. Seventy years after its initial destruction, a new, but very modest and plain temple was erected to the God of Israel.

Unfortunately, even this returned remnant eventually lost its identity, as it became infiltrated by the Greeks and later, by the Romans. By the time we arrive at the dawn of Yeshua's footsteps on the earth, Rome rules, with an iron hand, what is left of Israel. Jews, the faithful ones, look to the miracle God of the Bible to answer their prayers to be free from oppression, by sending the promised Messiah.

That Messiah, in turn, would regain Israel's freedom. In their thinking, under Messianic leadership they'd live in victory, as under the rule of King David. Israel, broken free from Rome, would, once again, be that rich and powerful nation from the past, well able to hold its own in the world in which they lived.

Unfortunately, the bulk of Israel looked at their *physical circumstances* to the problem which needed resolving. They defined and depicted their Messiah, not in balance with the spiritual, prophetic declarations of the Hebraic scriptures for that season, but rather by their need of freedom from Rome, their oppressors. Thus, they depicted their Messiah as a physical conquering king and his mission to free them from Roman oppression. At the time the Messiah arrived in the person of Yeshua, Israel's focus on deliverance from Rome was a priority. This precedence coloured their perception of their Messiah. Thus, due to the spiritual mission of Yeshua, on His first coming, they rejected Yeshua as the Messiah[26].

Nevertheless, into this scene came Yeshua, with His God-ordained mission to set the captives free; however, God's priority was spiritual. Here, in accordance with God's prophetic timetable, walked God's Messiah. His mission: *to redeem all humankind;* including both Jew and Gentile. Most, however, did not understand this aspect of God's plan.

From the very beginning of Yeshua's ministry, He made it very clear that His mission, which He lived out

---

[26] There are Jews, even today, who hold the same viewpoint. To them, Yeshua failed to set Israel free from Rome and thus, He could not be the Messiah. Jews need God's Hand to heal their blindness so they can see the reality of a spiritual Messiah.

before the Jews, was a *spiritual* mission. Yeshua's words, prophecies, and miracles worked to those ends, to help shift the people into a proper mindset, so they could receive their Messiah. First, however, they must focus their eyes away from warped teachings of the Pharisees, Sadducees, and Scribes. Then, they'd see the Messiah walking in their midst.

As Yeshua walked amongst the people of His day, His intentions were to present His Father, the God of Abraham, Isaac, and Jacob to His listeners, and to do His Father's will. His most important goal included their salvation and a relationship with them. This, however, escaped their understanding.

Through the Life of Yeshua, God showed Himself as real and powerful. Through Yeshua's works, God showed His power over nature, death, and demons, over sickness and disease, over lack and want. Time after time, God appeared in various circumstances to penetrate the darkness, shattering it completely, demonstrating resources far greater than His children could even dream. His Holy actions revealed His superiority to any challenges thrown at Him.

This is the God of the Bible!

This is the mighty One of Israel. His ability to implement His resources to resolve problems, situations, and predicaments, staggers the mind.

God's willingness to walk beside humankind and to help them through their troubles, staggers the mind, especially considering the terrible ways in which humankind responded to God.

Bible history clearly records, time after time, blatant refusals on the part of humankind to accept either God's Ways, His messages to repent or His warnings of pending judgments. Yet even though God's unique creation smugly retorted their insults before His Face, God remained available to mankind, with arms wide open to help and receive all who desire to come.

Bible history is dotted with encounters of God's mercy, compassion, grace, love, and understanding. That reality comes more to life in the Bible than in any other place. The God of the Bible reaches out to help each living person on earth *right where they live*.

> **God never expects the individual to come to Him as a perfect person.**

Nor does He expect that one who comes to Him to possess a pure and holy heart. He knows, apart from His Work within that person, such a state does not exist. God only asks a person to come to Him, *His Way*, as that way provides for all inadequacies of human beings.

Remember, this loving and compassionate God, Who fashioned humankind to fellowship with Him, reaches out to each living soul to come to Him, just as there are! Then, through the relationship between God as the Father, Yeshua as the Saviour, the Holy Spirit as the communication link, interaction occurs[27].

Each time one draws near to God and learns to share their heart with Him, inner, and outer transformations then take place. Thus, you have the basic formula for an awesome relationship for fellowship with the living God[28], the One Who created humankind *(and in particular, you, dear reader).*

Records of God's actions under the First and New Covenants portray Him as an amazing Being, with qualities humankind desperately needs. A look back, through the pages of this book, releases, to anyone who knows the reality of God, a pleasant aroma of outstanding qualities to describe the true and living God of the Bible.

---

[27] That is one amazing thing about the Salvation God provided! He designed it to meet us right where we are, and then, take us to where we need to go.

[28] Fellowship with God, as mentioned earlier, begins by accepting His plan of salvation. If you do not understand that salvation, please find Message of Salvation in the Appendix.

Looking specifically at the New Covenant writers, we see careful attention given to the miracles of Yeshua. These miracles show Yeshua in four major ways[29]:

- King of all Kings
- Son of Man
- Servant of God
- Son of God

Messiah, as the Gospel's describe Him, capably completed whatsoever was necessary to meet mankind's needs in every area, spiritual, mental, emotional, or physical needs. Repeatedly, Yeshua showed that with God, all things are possible and so four men, anointed and appointed by God, set out to record the events.

Matthew, Mark, Luke, and John had a target audience, a purpose, a plan, and a pointer directed straight towards God's character and person as seen in Yeshua. Each author showed God at work, through Yeshua. Matthew showed Him as the promised Messiah and King of Israel, Who was the fulfilment of the scriptures. Mark displayed Him as a willing servant, Who loved Jews and Gentiles. Luke penned Yeshua clearly as the Son of God. Lastly, John showed Him as the Son of Man. Together, these gospels show us that God is

---

[29] At the end of this chapter, for reference, please find an outline of the gospels.

greater, by far, over situations, circumstances, places, times, and seasons.

He is always, and always will be, more than able, to resolve all problems of humankind, including the ones mankind deems as impossible. His resources to do so are inexhaustible, unlimited, and infinite!

BEFORE SECTION 2:

THIS BOOK'S APPROACH TO MIRACLES:

As we examine the miracles of Yeshua, our source of reference must stem from no other source than the writings of the Apostles. Each Apostolic author, with their underlying theme for writing, as well as a target audience, presents Messiah to every aspect of humanity. Thus, we'll highlight each target audience, as well as the main thrust of the gospel. In that way, we'll draw from the scriptures *their original intent* and thus, better apply them to our own life. [30]

Thus, as we approach these miracles, we respect the Apostolic recordings of them, accepting them as God-breathed. As we draw conclusions, we do so, first, to aid our understanding of the God of the Bible, and secondly, to present solid ground for approaching

---

[30] You will find a chart recapping these at the end of this chapter.

Him, His Way and thus, properly implement His help on our behalf.

Miracles, which fall into the category of Power Over Nature, are the subject for this book. As we outline each miracle, we will investigate the following[31]:

- *Background Setting.* This helps to understand various aspects of each situation, circumstances, etc.
- *Operative Mindsets* Looking at the mindset of the characters involved in the miracle, helps us to recognize possible ways in which our mindsets may also be challenged. Then, we are positioned better to recognize a need for some changes in our thinking to align our lives with God's plans and purposes, and thus, receive our miracle.
- *Miracle Platform*: Once we determine the need, which is evidenced in the miracle setting, we easily identify how the scene was set for the miracle's entrance. In other words, we see the platform established, ready and waiting for God's Hand to move. This approach eliminates hard and fast rules of methodology, which in turn eradicates routine expectations of God, which tend to overlook the all-important *relationship aspect* with Him.
- *Revelation of God.* Each miracle, when God shows Himself as more than able, often against

---

[31] The order of the investigation may take a different form, dependent upon the miracle.

unsurmountable circumstances, presents aspects of God's character or abilities, ones we just might otherwise overlook. Reviewing these helps us to know God better and positions us to believe Him for greater things.

After these recaps, we'll bring forward some *possible insights* from the miracle, outline the miracle specifics, as well as surface and deeper meanings. All these things combined should give greater depth to understanding our God of miracles, how He thinks and why. Armed with that information, we should come just a little closer to receiving our own needed miracle!

Reflection Time:

Dear Reader, to get the best out of this book, at the end of each miracle in Section 2, you'll find a section entitled, "Reflections". Its purpose is to provide some additional thoughts, as well as give you time to reflect upon what you read, earlier. Simply put, it provides opportunity to reinforce some positive information about God.

As you reflect upon God's awesome ability to provide a solution for the situation under study situations, you set yourself up, *one more time*, to deposit information in a positive light to help you receive your own miracle, or the one you seek for another. Let this reflection time remind you that, whatever God has done for others, He will also do for you, too! [32]

---

[32] *Acts 10: 34-35 Then Peter opened his mouth, and said, Of a truth I perceive that God is **no respecter of persons**: But in every nation he that feareth him, and worketh righteousness, is accepted with him.*

Along those lines, dear reader, please deposit the following thoughts into your memory bank:
- Our God is truly the God of the Impossible. He awaits your invitation to be that to you! As you let each miracle speak to you, receive the gospel account as a personal love letter to you, from a trusted friend who would never steer you wrong. Keep focused on God, too, dear reader. Reach out to Him with a sincere heart to touch your life, right where you need Him to do so!
- Our God sent His Only Begotten Son, Yeshua, to walk upon the earth for your salvation, and in doing so, showed humankind the character of God. As you see Yeshua in action, as you encounter accounts of His compassion and mercy, as you see Him reach out to a person in need, know that is exactly what His Father would do. *As you see the heart of God responding to another, reach out towards Him so He may touch you. Allow Him to wrap you up in His wonderful arms of love. Receive from the gospel records what God desires for your life.*

In closing, dear reader, please remember what you read earlier:

learn to think like God.

Then, present your situation before the Lord as *a platform to show Himself strong.*

Willingly agree, dear reader, to align with His Counsel, exchanging your own counsel for His. Do this in all areas, especially in any places where you have unbelief, or thoughts of refusal to your requests, for whatever reason.

Beloved, you do your part, and God will do His! Look to Him for:

He is the God of unlimited resources!

He is the God of the Impossible

OUTLINE OF THE GOSPELS

MATTHEW [33]

Written to: *Messianic* Believers

MAJOR POINT: **Yeshua as King**

It was important to Matthew to prove that Yeshua was the Messiah, and as such, King of all Israel. All events Matthew chose to record, the miracles, the words, and prophecies written within the gospel pointed to Yeshua in such a way that all Jews, with an open mind to the truth, would see Yeshua as Messiah, and King of Israel.

MARK

Written to: *Gentile* Believers[34]

MAJOR POINT: **Yeshua as Servant**

When Mark wrote his gospel, it was to prove, from the very beginning, that Yeshua came as a Servant and lived amongst mankind. When listeners perceive this aspect of Yeshua, they will know their role is no different. Each one is to be a servant, first of the living God, and then towards those within and without the church.

---

[33] Originally, this book was written in Hebrew.

[34] There is only one Body of Messiah; however, in the early church it seemed that some churches were formed with the bulk of converted Jews, who, although one in Messiah, seemed disconnected from the converted Gentiles. The dynamics of each gospel reflected its recipients.

LUKE
Written to: *Messianic & Gentile* believers
MAJOR POINT: **Yeshua as the Son of Man**

Luke wrote to all people so they would understand that Yeshua was a human being, the perfect Son of God. It is imperative that believers receive both aspects of Yeshua's life, fully God, and fully mankind. Luke's gospel helps believers to see Him as such.

JOHN
Written to *Messianic & Gentile* believers
MAJOR POINT: **Yeshua as the Son of God**

All believers need to understand the gentleness of Yeshua and grasp the reality that God veiled Himself in flesh and walked amongst mankind, to show believers the nature and character of God. Like Luke, John knew the importance of seeing Yeshua as both God and mankind.

CANDIDATE FOR A MIRACLE

COURSE 304
(continued)

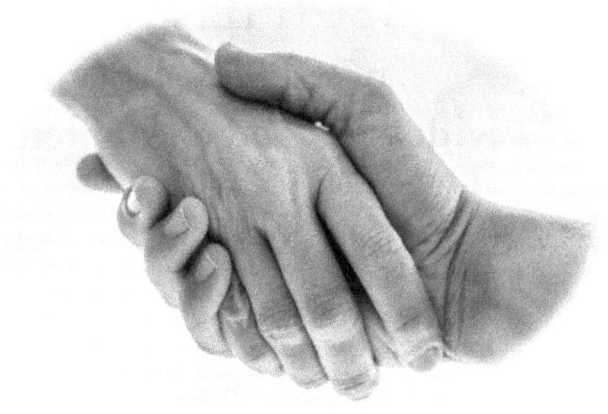

SECTION 2

RECEIVING THE MIRACLE

5

In receiving your miracle
Recognize God's Willingness

And the third day there was a marriage in Cana of Galilee; and the mother of Yeshua was there: 2 And both Yeshua was called, and his disciples, to the marriage. 3 And when they wanted wine, the mother of Yeshua saith unto him, They have no wine. 4 Yeshua saith unto her, Woman, what have I to do with thee? mine hour is not yet come. 5 His mother saith unto the servants, Whatsoever he saith unto you, do it. 6 And there were set there six waterpots of stone, after the manner of the purifying of the Jews, containing two or three firkins apiece. 7 Yeshua saith unto them, Fill the waterpots with water. And they filled them up to the brim. 8 And he saith unto them, Draw out now, and bear unto the governor of the feast. And they bare it. 9 When the ruler of the feast had tasted the water that was made wine, and knew not whence it was: (but the servants which drew the water knew;) the governor of the feast called the bridegroom, 10 And saith unto him, Every mankind at the beginning doth set forth good wine; and when men have well drunk, then that which is worse:

but thou hast kept the good wine until now. 11 This beginning of miracles did Yeshua in Cana of Galilee and manifested forth his glory; and his disciples believed on him.
John 2:1-11

WATER TURNED INTO WINE

This miracle takes place in the early days of Yeshua's ministry. However, just prior to the miracle, John the Baptist, called to witness to others about the arrival of the expected Messiah, saw Yeshua and called Yeshua the Lamb of God[35]. Verifying Yeshua as the expected one, two of John's followers decided to follow Yeshua. These two men, as well as others that Yeshua called to Himself, formed Yeshua's talmidim[36].

Now, Yeshua and His talmidim responded to an invitation to a wedding in Cana. Weddings in Yeshua's time functioned differently to weddings we hold today. To understand the miracle at Cana, we

---

[35] John 1:36

[36] A talmidim (pronounced tall ma deum) is a group of people who gather around a teacher to learn from that teacher. When they have learned what their leader or Master taught them, they leave, usually forming their own talmidim. This was an accepted and normal custom in the time of Yeshua.

must understand a little about the ancient wedding ritual of the Jews.

Ancient Wedding Rituals

In the time of Yeshua, and for centuries before, the Jews had a certain procedure to follow when a mankind desired to marry. First, the future groom would meet with the father of the intended bride. Together they would sit and write out what they called a "Ketubah" [37].

On the Ketubah, they plainly listed the rights for the bride, along with the basic responsibilities of the husband to provide for her. Two witnesses signed the Ketubah, and in the years to come, the Ketubah itself would act as a witness to ensure the husband fulfilled his part in the care of his wife. The bride, of course, also consented to this marriage contract.

To seal the Ketubah, (the contract) and make it legal, the future bride and groom, together, shared a cup of wine. From that point, onward, the Jewish Torah considered them betrothed, as a couple legally married. They would, however live in separate houses, not having any sexual union *until* the appointed day when the groom came for his bride.

---

[37] A Ketubah, then, is similar to what we might call a wedding contract today. Terms of the contract, once agreed to, demanded accountability.

This contract was so binding, only the death of one of the parties, or a legal divorce would break it.

After the couple signed the Ketubah and sealed it by sharing a cup of wine together, the groom went home to prepare a room for his wife, *most often*, in his father's house. In the meantime, until the wedding day arrived, neither bride nor groom knew the exact day and hour of their marriage. Only the groom's father knew the date, which he would set when he felt the time was right. Beginning then, at the signing of the Ketubah onward, the groom prepared a room for his bride in his father's house and the bride focused on preparing herself for the day of her groom's arrival.

Without notice, then, the bridegroom came, announcing his arrival at the last minute with the blast of a trumpet. All activities that previously occupied the bride immediately ended at the moment the trumpet announced the groom's arrival. Once, at the bride's house, the groom whisked his bride away to her new life, which began with a marriage consummation in the specially prepared place.

Outside that special chamber, the parents and other close relatives *began to gather and wait*. Guests, who earlier received invitations, when they heard the call to come to the banquet, ceased their activities, or if sleeping, arise from their bed and went to the celebration. Once arriving at the wedding, they dressed in a special wedding garment provided for them by the groom's father.

Once the bride and groom exited their special chamber, the celebration began[38], as they shared food and wine with family and friends. This joyous time of celebration marked their former life as over, and their married life as just begun.

BACKGROUND SETTING
Yeshua, with His talmidim, came to a certain Wedding Celebration. Miriam (Mary), the mother of Yeshua was there, also. Verse 9 speaks of the *bridegroom*, so we know that the
marriage consummation took place, earlier.

This newly married couple shared the joy of their oneness, celebrating their new life together, eating and drinking with their guests, *until a problem* threatened to spoil things. Insufficient provisions in that culture at that time, if not rectified, brought humiliation and shame to the groom. If not rectified, the couple would start their new life together in a very negative light.

---

[38] Three main elements make up the ancient Jewish wedding ceremony: 1) the Ketubah 2) the Consummation 3) the Wedding Feast.

OPERATIVE MINDSETS

In ancient times, in the Jewish mindset, "lack" was never a sign of blessing. On this special occasion, an inability to provide for your guests was a cultural no-no as lack of provision brought reproach. This problem must be resolved, but how?

Where would they get some wine? From whom would they get it? Their relatives and friends gathered with them, and the host meets the needs. That was the hospitality of the day!

Unlike our day, no stores stood ready with open doors to provide. In short, at this time, in this culture, it was humanly impossible for this embarrassing situation to go away by itself. Without a miracle, this bride and groom would experience a hug embarrassment, and enter married life with this ugly blot on their life.

MIRACLE PLATFORM

Remember, Miriam, Yeshua's mother, attended the wedding feast. We are not told in what capacity she came; however, many speculate that this wedding was a family affair *for Miriam*. In the story as John tells it from his eyewitness account, Miriam spoke to Yeshua, asking Him to resolve the matter.

Obviously, Miriam knew her son, Yeshua, had capabilities to take care of this problem. He would well understand the shame and disgrace ready to mar the life of the bride and groom. While Miriam had great faith and trust in the Lord, she probably had no idea of how Yeshua would resolve the matter. She only knew that He would. She approached Him without hesitation, knowing He would willingly resolve the matter, and thus, spare the newly married couple of such embarrassment.

Yeshua's first response, "Mine hour is not yet come", seems a refusal to help. However, Miriam did not receive it as such. Immediately, she looked at the servants and told him, "Whatever He tells you, do it[39]." While many look at Yeshua's comment as a direct corelation to the wedding at hand, it was not so.

Yeshua's comment made reference to His own marriage[40], which was not yet at hand. Probably, very acquainted with Yeshua's prophetic comments and not concerned with an immediate need to fully understand His Words, she advised the servants on how to respond. She knew in her heart Yeshua's willingness to help. Not doubting that willingness, she left the situation in His capable hands.

---

[39] John 2:5
[40] His own marriage comes at a future time (at another hour) when He returns and gathers His Bride unto Himself! More about this under the heading Miracle Specifics.

Her actions and her faith, she set up the platform for the miracle. Thus, with her words and actions, she opened the door for the entrance of God's Hand to change the situation and align it with God's provisional abilities. Her understanding of God's willingness to provide changed the situation from a catastrophe to a miracle.

REVELATION OF GOD

In this wedding setting, as in most Jewish weddings at that time, large urns filled with water stood nearby the wedding celebration. These large urns, kept especially for Pharisaic purifying rites for the marriage ceremony, earlier, held water. These empty water urns, Yeshua chose as the vessels to facilitate the miracle. Why He did that, we will see as we proceed to look at this miracle in greater depth. For now, let's look at this miracle to see how Yeshua revealed the Father as the ultimate provider.

Yeshua showed God's willingness as well as His ability to provide in a situation where mankind's short sightedness left him in a difficult place. This miracle, like other miracles, points us to our true source of provision. It also shows us God's compassion, love, mercy, and willingness to bless. Additionally, it shows His approval of the sanctity of marriage, as well as His desire to see the new life blessed.

A FEW MORE INSIGHTS

One for the reasons Yeshua used the empty water jugs for this miracle (beyond challenging the religious mindsets of the Pharisees), comes to light when we glean an understanding of a unique miracle that happened under the First Covenant. That miracle, which transpired many centuries prior to Yeshua's birth, many Jewish believers knew, as it marked the appearance of a prophet in their midst.

> 2 Kings 4:1-7
> "**1** ¶ Now there cried a certain woman of the wives of the sons of the prophets unto Elisha, saying, Thy servant my husband is dead; and thou knowest that thy servant did fear YeHoVaH: and the creditor is come to take unto him my two sons to be bondmen. **2** And Elisha said unto her, What shall I do for thee? tell me, what hast thou in the house? And she said, Thine handmaid hath not any thing in the house, save a pot of oil. **3** Then he said, Go, borrow thee vessels abroad of all thy neighbours, *even*. empty vessels; borrow not a few. **4** And when thou art come in, thou shalt shut the door upon thee and upon thy sons, and shalt pour out into all those vessels, and thou shalt set aside that which is full".
> "**5** So she went from him and shut the door upon her and upon her sons, who brought the vessels to her; and she poured out. **6** And it came to pass, when the vessels were full, that she said unto her

son, Bring me yet a vessel. And he said unto her, *There is* not a vessel more. And the oil stayed. 7 Then she came and told the mankind of God. And he said, Go, sell the oil, and pay thy debt, and live thou and thy children of the rest".

In those days, creditors often saw children as chattel. They would take the children from those indebted to them, sell them into slavery and keep the sum as payment for borrowed funds. What an atrocity for the widow woman to face!

In those days, a widow woman's son was incredibly important to her ability to stay alive. Sons worked and held property, thus they provided for their family, which included aging parents, especially widows. Besides the horror of her sons being sold into slavery, the poor widow woman would eventually die without food, clothing, and shelter. This was a desperately grave situation and one not too easily resolved unless God performed a miracle! With that hope in mind, she went to the prophet Elisha.

After hearing about her plight, Elisha asked her a question saying, "Tell me, what do you have in the house?[41]" When Elisha discovered that she had some oil in her home, he knew what substance God would use to provide income for the woman. Elisha, using

---

[41] This paraphrases the King James language in verse 2

God's Wisdom, told the widow woman to borrow many vessels, (bottles) from her neighbours and then take the vessels with her into the inner chamber of her house, along with her sons. Upon entering her house, she was to shut the door.

When behind her closed door, with only she and her sons present, she poured out the little bit of oil. Miraculously, God multiplied the oil until it filled every bottle she borrowed. Bringing the filled vessels to Elisha, he told her to sell that oil and use the money to pay off her debts. [42]

So many good lessons of faith spring forth when looking at this wonderful miracle! One specific lesson lies in the fact that **God used what the widow woman had available.** God did not advise the use of something that was beyond her reach. If He did that, it would make the miracle unattainable for her. *No, God chose to use something at hand, something easily within her grasp, thus making the miracle's fulfilment near and very possible.*

Of course, the widow woman had a part to play, but that part lay in her obedience to the instructions. Without doing her part, the miracle would slip away from her. However, her faith in God and trust in the

---

[42] Obviously, Elisha trusted her to return the borrowed vessels to the neighbours.

prophet's words kicked in. Her obedience saw the fulfilment of the miracle and resolution to her distressing situation.

Returning now to look back at the wedding in Cana, Yeshua also used *that which was available,* namely the empty water pots and water[43]. Yeshua used the same principle as Elisha and thus *set up the situation to succeed.* A servant at the feast obeyed His orders and as he did, the miracle became a reality.

MIRACLE SPECIFICS

Remember, Yeshua's comment to His mother, which of course, His disciples heard: "My hour is not yet come".[44] To fully understand Yeshua's comment, as well as another message of the miracle beneath the surface, we need to remember that Yeshua, at other times, referred to His time on the cross as His hour. For example, looking at the ordeal ahead of Him, *(becoming sin and going to the cross and all it entailed),* Yeshua prayed, "If it were possible, the hour might pass from him".[45]

---

[43] At this time, Yeshua also hit hard against the Pharisees for their mankind-made rituals. In other words, Yeshua slammed hard against the Pharisaical practices and commandments which added to and took away from the Word of God. This is another extremely important aspect of this miracle.
[44] John 2:4b (paraphrased into modern English)
[45] Mark 14:35b

It was important to Yeshua that, before and after the miracle, those present, especially His disciples, would look at the marvellous sign or wonder of the water turned into wine, and learn its deeper meaning. His disciples, who one day would be the carriers of the gospel, must understand His purpose for coming to earth. He came as their Saviour, the One God called to save all humankind.

Keeping the message of Yeshua's purpose in mind, we see the way Yeshua thought of Himself[46]. We know from other scripture passages that Yeshua spoke of Himself as the *Bridegroom*. To bring this underlying message to mind, using some of the analogies of the Jewish wedding feast, we see the following:

- Yeshua declared Himself as the Bridegroom. *(The sum of born again, spirit filled believers, over the ages, living for God alone, makes up the Bride.)*
- Each written Ketubah set out the conditions of the marriage, such as the rights of the Bride, as well as the husband's commitment to provide, care for and love her. Yeshua's Ketubah is seen within the New Covenant outlined as the believer's inheritance. The Bridal price was

---

[46] 1 John 4: 9 "In this was manifested the love of God toward us, because that God sent his only begotten Son into the world, that we might live through him. 10 Herein is love, not that we loved God, but that he loved us, and sent his Son to be the propitiation for our sins".

- paid at the cross and set in agreement long before Yeshua went to the cross.
- Yeshua told His disciples "In my Father's house are many mansions: if it were not so, I would have told you. I go to prepare a place for you".[47] Here is the part where the Groom goes away to prepare the Bridal Chamber. Then, when the Father says, "Go", He comes for His Bride.
- Until Yeshua's return, the Bride's role is to be ready for her groom, ensuring at a moment's notice, she is prepared to leave with her Bridegroom at the trumpet call.

Looking back then at the miracle of Cana, perceiving Yeshua as the Bridegroom, and the crucifixion, which He called, "His Hour", we see more of what Yeshua meant, when He said to Miriam, "What has this to do with Me? My hour has not yet come." First, the wedding at Cana was not the wedding of Yeshua. His wedding was yet to come! At the "hour" of His crucifixion, Yeshua would pay the Bridal Price by giving of Himself. After His resurrection and ascension, He returned to His Father's house, just the same as any Bridegroom, there to wait until the Father released Him to go for His Bride.

---

[47] John 14:2

These lessons, at the time of the wedding feast of Cana, were veiled within the customs of the times. Yeshua's disciples and His mother too, did not understand the meaning of the words as Yeshua spoke them, but later, after His Resurrection and Ascension into glory, when God opened their minds to the New Covenant, they understood.

This miracle at Cana, Yeshua ensured by His words, would hold fruitful meaning to His disciples, long after the wedding ended. While His disciples saw the sign and wonder of the water turned to wine, and while they knew a great prophet was in their midst, their focus was not to be upon the miracle! No, in time to come, they must think about the stirring comments of Yeshua, pondering His words within the setting of *the New Covenant* inaugurated by Yeshua.

A SURFACE MEANING
In this miracle, we see an important need met: *a bridegroom and his bride saved from embarrassment.* While this miracle was done quietly, it affected many people:

- **the wedding couple:** Perhaps, in years to come, as they reflected upon their plight on their wedding day, they'd remember their almost embarrassment, yet cherish the bountiful blessing of God's goodness to them.
- **Miriam, Yeshua's mother:** Miriam was confident that God did not desire embarrassment for this young married couple. Perhaps she recalled her

own marriage and its circumstances. Perhaps her trust in Yahweh Jireh, (the Lord her provider) was working here. After all, she knew God as mighty!
- **the servants and ruler of the feast**: Stewards obeyed the orders of Yeshua. Perhaps they, more than any other, was affected, as they knew what substance they put into the water jugs and what substance came out. The master of the feast was impressed, and not likely to forget the wine from that feast, including the order in which it was served.
- **the Disciples**: This occasion showed them that there was a great prophet in their midst, and they knew Him! Perhaps they asked themselves, "is he that which is to come?"

Scripture tells us none of these things, however. It merely records the outer actions of some of the characters involved and concludes with the important fact that Yeshua's disciples believed on Him.

A DEEPER MEANING
To perceive this miracle's depth, we must first look at the impact it made on the disciples.

John records that in Chapter 2, verse 11

John 2:11
> "This beginning of miracles did Yeshua in Cana of Galilee and manifested forth his glory; *and his disciples believed on him*".

Many people at that time, including Yeshua's disciples, had certain ideas of the Messiah. Yeshua, declared by John the Baptist, as the Lamb of God, now had certain followers convinced of His favour with God.

Through this miracle, Yeshua *challenged their mindset* to think of Him differently than before the miracle, and probably differently in their viewpoint of the capabilities and role of the Messiah. These disciples must not only see a teacher and a prophet working miracles, but they must *learn* the Ways of God. That information would go a long way as they walked with God until the ends of their lives.

Yeshua used empty water jugs; ones earlier used for a ceremonial purification rite. In time, the disciples realized that Yeshua washed them clean, but not through any manmade or ritualistic activities. Yeshua said to them,

John 15: 3
> 3 Now *ye are clean* through the word which I have spoken unto you.

Sanctification, that act of being set apart for God, comes not by ritual or outside cleansing with water. Yeshua's sanctification of His Bride, each believer in Him, comes by faith through the works Yeshua completed on the cross. It is a result of those works that one is washed cleaned. Filling the empty jars with water pointed to something the New Covenant alone would provide. Yeshua put it this way,

> John 7:38-39
> "38 He that believeth on me, as the scripture hath said, out of his belly shall flow rivers of living water. 39 (But this spake he of the Spirit, which they that believe on him should receive: for the Holy Ghost was not yet given; because that Yeshua was not yet glorified.)"

After Calvary, all believers in Yeshua are clean, each one aligned to receive the fresh water of the Holy Ghost from Whom comes a flow of living waters. In this, there is also another symbolic thing which cannot be overlooked, and it is this: *when the earthen vessel, (saved humankind) empties itself of all its own efforts and receives the provision of God, they are filled with new wine.* This is the best wine left for last!

Looking back to the disciples gathered at that wedding, each one needed to look at Yeshua, in the light of Who He was and why He came. This they did when Yeshua ate the last Passover with them:

> 1 Corinthians 11:24-26
> "24 And when he had given thanks, he break it, and said, Take, eat this is my body, which is broken for you: this do in remembrance of me. 25 After the same manner also he took the cup, when he had supped, saying, This cup is the new testament in my blood: this do ye, as oft as ye drink it, in remembrance of me. 26 For as often as ye eat this bread, and drink this cup, ye do shew the Lord's death till he come."

If we look deep enough into this miracle, we see that for His disciples to understand, to truly grasp the significance of Yeshua and what God said to them through Him, *they must allow their mindset to change.* They must look past their view of the Messiah, which was rather narrow due to the concealed revelation about the Messiah. They must embrace the view of God, and from that view see God's intentions to cleanse humankind.

> 1 John 1:7
> "7 But if we walk in the light, as he is in the light, we have fellowship one with another, and the blood of Yeshua Ha' Maschiach his Son cleanseth us from all sin."

Yeshua, during "His Hour", (the time of His Crucifixion), changed forever how believers come to God for cleansing. External washings, rituals and the like, will never bring to mankind the cleansing needed for God to see them as clean. We cannot wash away our sins any other way than with the Blood of the Lamb. This the author of Hebrews boldly proclaimed when writing this passage:

> Hebrews 9:13-14
> "13 For if the blood of bulls and of goats, and the ashes of a heifer sprinkling the unclean, sanctifieth to the purifying of the flesh: 14 How much more shall the blood of Yeshua Ha' Maschiach, who through the eternal Spirit offered himself without spot to God, purge your conscience from dead works to serve the living God?"

Such thoughts as these challenged the minds of those bound by the First Covenant, as well as those minds trapped by tradition and religion. Often, if humankind are to receive from God, their mindsets are challenged and must change! This miracle challenged many as we have seen thus far. In the following paragraphs, more mindset changes are recorded.

MINDSETS CHALLENGED

Yeshua challenged the disciples present at the miracle of Cana, inviting them to think of Him, past the idea of a teacher, their Master. He needed to stretch them in their thinking, which He eventually did, helping His Disciples to realize that He was God incarnate, their Messiah, fully God and fully mankind.

In that culture, a Rabbi, prior to taking disciples of his own, was himself a disciple. Earlier, prior to the career as a Rabbi, that person subjected himself beneath the teaching of a learned mankind, one that was well respected. He stayed under that tutelage until he earned the respect of the teacher.

Once the teacher felt that he taught his student all he could, he laid his hands on that student and commissioned him to be a Rabbi, sent to carry on teaching the same as they received. In that way, *the new Rabbi received the authority to teach from the former Rabbi who tutored him.* After that graduation from learning, the student, now the teacher, found their own disciples and the cycle repeated itself.

Looking at Yeshua, Who preferred His talmidim to call Him, Master or Moreh (meaning teacher) and not Rabbi, something was very different. First of all, Yeshua never tutored under a Rabbi. He was God mentored! Secondly, regarding His walk with God and the authority He carried, that came from God, Who anointed Him. Also, as we recall the reason for John's gospel,[48] Yeshua's first miracle is proof that

---

[48] To show Yeshua as fully God and fully mankind.

Yeshua is not an ordinary mankind. Indeed, John wanted his audience to understand that the miracle of genuinely changing water into wine, was only possible through the power of God.[49]

John's gospel furnishes many more proofs of Yeshua's deity and humanity, but this first miracle, to the apostles, was a convincing act that caused John to write:

> John 2: 11 (note part in italics and bolded)
> 11 This beginning of miracles did Yeshua in Cana of Galilee and manifested forth his glory; and ***his disciples believed on him.***

A FEW ADDED THOUGHTS

Yeshua's disciples, the ones present at the wedding at Cana, as well as the others who came along side later, must all learn that Yeshua was more than a Moreh (teacher), and far more than their idea of the Messiah. All Yeshua's disciples must learn to look outside the box of what they knew. Each one must allow the Holy

---

[49] Magicians have a trick, today, where they claim to change water into wine. In glass #1, they have the water. In glass # 2, they have an invisible chemical. As they pour the water from one glass into the glass with the chemical, the water changes colour to look like wine. As long as no one tastes the so-called wine, they get away with their trick. Yeshua's water into wine, however, was the real thing, and so much so that the head of the feast commented on its excellent quality.

Spirit to shatter the perimeters of their thinking to enable a God-inspired, God developed view of the Messiah.

Beginning with this early group of disciples at the wedding of Cana, and moving throughout His relationship with all of them, Yeshua would often change the way they thought, how they perceived God, as well as the assignment of Messiah. After Yeshua's death, burial, resurrection, and ascension, the Holy Spirit would broaden the minds of the disciples to receive Yeshua in the capacity in which He came and the New Covenant which He inaugurated.

This challenge to the apostles established thinking, *the stretching process of learning to think above the mind of mankind, to utilize the wisdom of God,* pressed hard against the foundational and fixed mindsets already established by their years of living. Challenges of this kind pervaded the apostles, throughout their time with Messiah before the cross, and certainly after as well. To take the message of Salvation to others, fulfilling the Great Commission, also meant leaning to forsake the wisdom of mankind for the wisdom of God; to reject walking in the flesh for walking in the power of the Holy Spirit.

This same stretching experience, **this same challenge of the replacing the wisdom of mankind,** await all disciples of Yeshua, from the cross onward. Each believer, like the Apostles, must learn that, in all our circumstances and in every situation, God is far greater and does things His way! Each believer from Yeshua's disciples onward must shift gears in thinking from human thoughts to embrace God's thoughts. Each believer must realise a possibility exists for them to soar past their present thinking, no matter its source, to embrace God's viewpoint, which, when summarized says, "with God all things are possible".

Every situation, no matter how difficult, no matter how impossible to the mind of mankind, stands as a potential or waiting miracle. Each and every impossible situation potentially has power to draw God into it to release His mighty authority and transform that situation, forever.

Each believer must come to terms with the solution waiting in the wings. That solution, God already created and designed to be met with God's resolve. To receive the solution requires thinking outside of our box! It requires moving past our human understanding to allow the Holy Spirit to show us the depths of possibilities with God! Once we allow the Spirit to minister to our thoughts and help us align with those of the Creator, we are but one step away from the needed miracle.

In receiving the miracle, just remember God's willingness to give the miracle, as well as help you align your thinking to receive it!

Reflection Time:

Believers, everywhere, just like Yeshua's first disciples, experience struggles when asked to release certain mindsets to grasp the truths the Holy Spirit brings to them. Adjusting, or even, at times, discarding religious mindsets which the Holy Spirit shows as contrary to God's Word, presents challenges for which many are unprepared. It seems that the hardest mindsets to change are those formed by religious beliefs, many of which improperly rest on certain scripture passages taken out of context, which the Holy Spirit wishes to realign. Some beliefs which people received over the centuries, unfortunately, rest on anything but scripture. Many are culturally acceptable but not biblically, correct. Therefore, they are difficult to perceive and problematic to change.

Yeshua, in His first miracle, wanted others to see the larger picture, to open their minds to the Messiah, *as God ordained Him* to be, not necessarily *as mankind perceived Him.* Yeshua ensured, too, that onlookers were not taken off course to follow the direction of the sign or wonder. Rather, He wanted their minds aligned with the truth of why He came.

Yeshua knew something many believers forget. *God desires that we don't just see and know His Works, but rather, we seek and learn God's ways.*

Knowing this will take the believer, past the surface relationship with God and move them into deep waters instead. There, the believer finds the truest satisfaction of a life lived before the face of the Almighty. From that place, deep in communion with God, the believer finds their best friend, their faithful, loving, caring and responsive Creator able to sustain them through the trials and tribulations that often touch the life of a believer.

Yeshua's followers, His disciples then and His disciples now, must follow Him into places where *a surface relationship* simply will not cut it.

No relationship with God rests solely on signs and wonders.

Relationships must go deeper, touching the character of the One capable of performing those signs and wonders.

Each believer choosing to walk with Yeshua, must recognize that while Yeshua is the Messiah, in accordance with the focus of the gospel of John, He is also the Son of God. He is deity, and His mission, His goal, the reason for His birth, is to bring all humankind into a relationship with God, that begins here upon the earth, but lasts an eternity.

Yeshua took great pains to present an in-depth relationship with His Father and taught His disciples to reach for such as well. This kind of relationship with God was not only of great personal value, but it also afforded the necessary foundation to reach out to the world and bring forth God's message of salvation. Each disciple who was loyal to God, the Father, and loyal to Yeshua, *who embraced the Messianic vision and mission, and through the power of the Holy Spirit,* kept the message alive. Certainly, that all important message endures, affecting every generation until Yeshua returns.

We must also fully realize that the "relationship", the place of communion with God, is meat for our souls and joy for our days. We need not shy away from the trials and tribulations of life, or the costs paid to live as a Christian in a world where many prefer our non-existence.

Rather, we need to step into the deep waters with God. We must, with courage and strength, press into the place where the relationship with God stands paramount above the signs and wonders of His Presence. Like the early apostles, we must let that good foundation form, and project us to preach it to every creature!

Dear one, reflect on these things. Ask the Lord to help you, and if you need help in embracing the larger picture, He stands with arms wide open to receive and help you.

Regarding your relationship, ask the Lord to give you clarity of your truest desires, meaning, do you truly long to know His ways and form the deepest possible relationship with Him.

Ask the Lord to help you *with mindsets, especially the ones that He perceives needs changing.*

Above all dear reader, recognize His willingness to walk with you throughout every day of your life, no matter the circumstances, problems or solutions needed. Remember, God stands for you and not against you. He stands ready and waiting for you to reach out and say, "Here I am". Teach me Your Ways. Help me to follow!

6

In receiving your miracle
Recognize God's Sovereignty

*A*nd it came to pass, that, as the people pressed upon him to hear the word of God, he stood by the lake of Gennesaret, **2** And saw two ships standing by the lake: but the fishermen were gone out of them, and were washing their nets. **3** And he entered into one of the ships, which was Simon's, and prayed him that he would thrust out a little from the land. And he sat down and taught the people out of the ship. **4** Now when he had left speaking, he said unto Simon, Launch out into the deep, and let down your nets for a draught. **5** And Simon answering said unto him, Master, we have toiled all the night, and have taken nothing: nevertheless, at thy word I will let down the net. **6** And when they had this done, they enclosed a great multitude of fishes: and their net brake. **7** And they beckoned unto their partners, which were in the other ship, that they should come and help them. And they came, and filled both the ships, so that they began to sink. **8** When Simon Peter saw it, he fell down at Yeshua's knees, saying, Depart from me; for I am a sinful mankind, O Lord. **9** For he was astonished, and all that were with him, at the draught of the *fishes which they had taken:* **10** *And so was also James, and John, the sons of Zebedee, which were partners with Simon. And Yeshua said unto Simon, Fear not; from henceforth thou shalt catch men.* **11** *And when they had brought their ships to land, they forsook all, and followed him".*

Luke 5:1-11

A LARGE CATCH OF FISH

BACKGROUND SETTING

In this scripture passage from Luke 5, the writer mentions Lake Gennesaret. Today, most people call that body of water the Sea of Galilee. This body of water is the largest fresh water source in Israel, and interestingly, it is the lowest freshwater lake on earth measuring 209 meters (686 feet) below sea level.[50] This body of water is fed by some underground springs, but mostly through the Jordan River which flows from North to South right through it. At its deepest part, this body of water is approximately 43 meters (141 feet).

Over the centuries, the Sea of Galilee has worn many name tags, amongst them, its modern name, Kinneret

---

[50] These facts obtained from Wikipedia, online.

Lake. [51] From this body of water, ancient fishermen made a good living, catching basically three types of fish. Today we know those species as Sardines, Barbels, (a carp like, freshwater fish) and Musht, better known as St. Peter's fish.[52]

While fishing on the Sea of Galilee, many a fisherman has lost their life due to storms, which grow quickly. They can be quite fierce, with rather high winds. Some scientists attribute the rise of these storms to the fact of the Lake's location. It settles deep into the Rift Valley. That area has known earth tremors and quakes, and in former years, it is suspected also to have experienced volcanic activity.

This body of water is mentioned often throughout the gospels, where it speaks of various activities, including teachings of Yeshua on its shores, as well as miracles happening in its depths.[53] It was a very important body of water then, and it is equally valuable today. Of course, to avid students of the Bible, it also holds special interests.

---

[51] Authorities state this name came from the Tanakh, appearing first in Numbers 34:11 and showing up in passages in Deuteronomy, Joshua and 1 Kings.
[52] The Sea of Galilee is off limits to fishermen today.
[53] If you should ever have a chance to go to Israel, dear reader, try not to miss a ship ride on Lake Kinneret. Each tourist ship tries to make it a wonderful experience.

OPERATIVE MINDSETS

In Yeshua's time, as in generations prior, *(and even into modern times[54])* many people earned their living from fishing in Lake Kinneret. Early in the morning, in those days, as one walked along the edge of the lake, they would see evidence of the fishermen bringing in their catch from the previous night. First, they'd sort through the fish, quickly, then send it to market. Next, they'd wash their nets.

One day, as Yeshua walked along the shoreline, He saw a fisherman, named Simon Peter, standing on the shore of Lake Kinneret, washing his nets. Unfortunately, Peter returned with empty nets after his night-long fishing trip. Since fishing was Peter's livelihood, this lack of a catch meant Peter and his family would lack income to provide for the necessities of life. It is quite probable that Peter was disappointed and frustrated, as would be any normal fisherman.

Upon seeing Peter, Yeshua stepped into Peter's ship, and asked to be put out a little distance from shore. Peter complied. Yeshua preceded to teach the crowds of people gathered at Lake Kinneret. When Yeshua finished His discourse, with the crowds still listening, He asked Peter to put the ship out into the deeper waters and then put down his nets.

---

[54] The government of Israel, in 2010 passed a law forbidding fish to be removed from Lake Kinneret.

Peter reminded Yeshua that he had been out all night and caught nothing. Peter's normal instinct, *his normal manner of thinking*, would be to forget it. It is simply a waste of time to go out again. It is probably better to go home to bed. Peter, however, had been an attendant at the wedding at Cana. Even in this short amount of time, Peter learned Yeshua was different than other Rabbis. Willingly, Peter did as Yeshua asked. In that moment, he opened the door wide for a miracle.

MIRACLE PLATFORM

Peter, as well as his fishing companions, employed the best methods of fishing for their time in history. So, after a night of disappointing fishing, mankind's wisdom did not dictate going back out at a time when you're most likely not to succeed. Nevertheless, *Peter bowed to Yeshua's request*. If Peter, instead, jeered at Yeshua's suggestion, or chose another course to follow, or if he argued with Yeshua, nothing miraculous would happen. With Yeshua already in the ship, the major ingredient for the miracle was already in place! The next step, Peter took, pushing the little fishing craft back into Lake Kinneret, aiming for the deeper water. At that point, Peter set the platform for the miracle to occur.

So great was the catch of fish that Peter, as well as his fishing partners, loaded the catch in their ships to the point of sinking. The God of Abraham, Isaac, and

Jacob, once again, smiled on Israel, giving them a great prophet ... and they, being privileged to know Him, left everything, and followed Him. After all, they had a little taste of their God showing Himself as with them, alive in their midst!

REVELATION OF GOD

Peter, through this miracle, experienced a revelation of God that he'd not soon forget, and also a revelation of himself. He saw God's hand as provider when he received the catch of fish, however, he caught a glimpse of the mankind of God in the ship with Him. That glimpse helped Peter to see himself in a new light, confessing with his mouth that he was indeed a sinful mankind.

> Luke 5: 8-9
>
> . **8** When Simon Peter saw *it*, he fell down at Yeshua's knees, saying, Depart from me; for I am a sinful mankind, O Lord. **9** For he was astonished, and all that were with him, at the draught of the fishes which they had taken:

Peter. thought his sinfulness was reason enough to remove himself from Yeshua's company, however, Yeshua responded with these words, "Fear not; from henceforth thou shalt catch men."[55] This revelation of God was key to Peter's acknowledgement of who he

---

[55] Luke 5:10

was, and what he needed. That need was far more than fish, indeed, for Peter needed a Saviour.

A FEW MORE INSIGHTS

In looking at the specifics of this miracle, we note, once again, that Yeshua used something available and at Peter's disposal, *namely tools of Peter's livelihood, his ship and net.* While Yeshua's practicality set the scene for receiving the miracle, Peter must move in the direction to receive it. Peter must take responsibility and do something, obeying the given instructions, which seemed contrary to the expertise of fishermen. To attain his miracle, then, Peter's training as a fisherman must take a back seat. He must listen to the Teacher, Whose trade *was not fishing!* Peter, as all those who receive a miracle from God, must look past the circumstance to the One Who alone can produce the miracle, to the Lord Who is sovereign and supreme!

Setting aside his own mindset, Peter followed the instructions of Yeshua and set out to receive his miracle. [56]

MIRACLE SPECIFICS

As Peter followed the instructions of Yeshua, taking the ship out in the deep to throw down his nets, his

---

[56] For extra reading, go to 2 Kings 5:11-15 and read the account of a mankind with leprosy, healed after following the instructions of the prophet.

obedience resulted in a catch of fish so great that the nets were breaking. Peter called to his fishing partners still along the shoreline. "Come and help" was the order of the day, and so, Peter's fishing partners came.

How amazing that the catch filled both ships and to such a capacity that they began to sink down into the water under the weight. It was still early enough in the day to return to shore, sort and send the fish out to the waiting merchants. Surely such an exceptional catch would provide an exceptional income, more than enough to meet the needs of the fishermen in the ships. However, please note the response:

Luke 5:11

> **11** And when they had brought their ships to land, they forsook all, and followed him".

A SURFACE MEANING
On the surface, we see that Yeshua, through the spoken Word, met, *beyond expectation,* the needs of Peter and his partners. All they needed to do was agree with Yeshua's command, abandoning their mindsets to obey Him.

Following Yeshua's instructions, moving out into the deeper waters, one might wonder what thoughts went through Peter's mind. Earlier, in his beginning relationship with this Teacher from Nazareth, Peter saw a bridegroom and his bride receive a miracle that saved them great embarrassment, as Yeshua turned water turned into wine. That was then, but now, a fruitless night of fishing was an entirely different situation. How would Yeshua resolve this current problem? What could He do in the deeper waters of the Lake, when Peter and his companions caught nothing?

On the surface, we see that Peter received a miracle catch, but to do so, he left something behind! Truly, his immediate need on the surface, hid the spiritual need, which came to the surface. We see it plainly and clearly as Peter acknowledged his sinfulness. From that recognition of his greater need, to forsake his sinful life, Peter forsakes all to answer the call to follow Yeshua. Peter looked for something real in a relationship with God. He saw it in the call to follow Yeshua!

Another more surface message comes, as we realize that *with obedience comes blessings*. Blessings come, but not always the way one expects! In this situation, Peter *loaned* Yeshua his ship to use as a stage to speak to the gathering crowds. After Yeshua taught, He determined to bless Peter beyond that mankind's wildest dreams. The following scripture describes both the type of blessing Yeshua gave, and the blessing these fishermen received:

Luke 6:38

38 Give, and it shall be given unto you; good measure, pressed down, and shaken together, and running over, shall men give into your bosom[57]. For with the same measure that ye mete withal it shall be measured to you again

No one *ever* out gives God!

A DEEPER MEANING

To grasp the deeper meaning of this miracle, we need to follow Yeshua's comments a little closer. When responding to Peter's statement in verse 9, *"Depart from me, for I am a sinful mankind, O Lord"*, Yeshua said Peter should not fear. Peter did not say he *should* run away from the Lord. Peter, rather, told Yeshua *to depart from his company*. What did Peter experience with Yeshua in this encounter?

In recognizing his own sinfulness, Peter first came to recognize Yeshua as a mankind of God, but not just an ordinary one which operated in the religious system of the day. This mankind Yeshua did things like the prophets of old. This kind of mankind, Peter's generation did not normally see. Seeing Yeshua's connection with God, Peter thought that he should not be defiled by the likes of Peter. Peter's reactions show

---

[57] This expression refers to the front part of a garment where one could tuck and carry things. The entire scripture refers to a bountiful supply, astounding and far more than just enough.

fear of not be accepting for the person he was *a sinful mankind*. Hence Yeshua's words, "do not be afraid, settled the matter.

While feelings of unworthiness may accompany an encounter with God, to embrace fear as a motive for answering the call of God builds a weak foundation for answering that call. When God calls, He desires His followers to see His greatness for sure, but feelings of unworthiness or dread of God leave room to work contrary to building a relationship.

Holding respect for God must be there, however, God prefers responses from a heart of love for Him, His Word, and His Ways. Of this same thing the Psalmist speaks.

Psalm 32:8-9

> 8 I will instruct thee and teach thee in the way which thou shalt go: I will guide thee with my eye. 9 Be ye not as the horse, [or] as the mule, [which] have no understanding: whose mouth must be held in with bit and bridle, lest they come near unto thee.

In following the ways of God, as verse 8 speaks, one must not be as the horse or as the mule, who does things by direction of a bit in their mouth. One must willingly follow God from a heart that understands Who He is and from that understanding, they remain faithful and obedient to Him. They do not serve God because of a forcible bit restraining them from going their own way.

Simply put, God prefers mankind follow Him from a heart of love. Such a heart develops over time, desiring to please Him. These followers know His Ways and understand them as the best for their lives.

Indeed, God invites one to follow Him, not demanding it! He makes a way for one to follow Him, too, including furnishing the grace required to implement the necessary changes in that person's life. One must simply look past *their* goals and expectations of their own life and reach for the *goals and expectations* on God's heart. In love, one yields their will to God for His greater purpose.

Yeshua clearly tells Peter of a new goal for his life, *a career change*. From then on, just as Peter used the tools of his net and ship to catch fish, he now has opportunity to spread a different net in the sea of life. The catch *is souls,* their destiny, the Kingdom of God. Thus, Peter, as well as the others Yeshua calls, brings the message of salvation to waiting ears, desperate for truth.

Peter, who made the needed shift, no longer toiled for his own labours, but instead, laboured for souls. This shift demonstrates yet another powerful lesson we must consider. Peter, a married mankind, must have provision for his family. Now God, through whatever means He decided, promises provision for His followers.

As they leave their means of earning a living for the sole purposes of following Yeshua, they know they can put their trust in God to meet all their needs, and not just adequately provide, but provision above and beyond their expectations. Indeed, God reigns, supreme over all things, and well able to provide for His servants.

In this catching of souls, from God's perspective, we see that God, because of His love for the lost, supplies the needs of His workers, as they willingly become God's voice, to call to humankind to accept God's invitation to repent and enter His Kingdom. That call, which translates souls from death to life, is so very important to God, that nothing is too much trouble for God to redeem a soul. He looks for those willing to go "fish" for them!

MINDSETS CHALLENGED
Peter's first mindset challenge came when asked to return to the lake, sail into the deeper waters, and there, lower his nets. Perhaps his tired body preferred sleep! This we are not told, only that he agreed to Yeshua's invitation to put the tiny craft back into the Lake.

Another mindset challenge came after the catch of fish. Peter, as a husband in his day, knew their responsibility of providing for their family. Up to the point in time, moments before Yeshua invited Peter to launch out into the deep with Him, Peter cared for his family with a fishing career. This encounter with Yeshua called Peter away from his fishing career, *but it could not call him away from providing for his family*. Through the miracle, however, Yeshua showed God's ability to provide for the family, far better than Peter did on his own.

Peter *(as well as James and John, the sons of Zebedee and as the gospels share, others)* shifted their mindset of provision coming *solely through their own ability*, to a solid trust in God for provision, through *whatever means He chose*. How the Lord provided would, of course, be specific to different situations; however, the new dynamics of trusting God to provide required a definite change in mindset.

A FEW ADDED THOUGHTS

On that same line regarding provision, in the epistles, we read that Paul, the Apostle, made tallits[58] for a living, the sales of which funded his missionary journeys. Other early, first-century leaders received income from believers in churches which they founded. Believers also helped each other, as well as

---

[58] Translations say "tents"; however, we know from a study on Hebraic roots, that Paul did not make tents for people to dwell in, but rather "prayer tents" or "tallit's".

the poor. Paul, the Apostle, summed this matter up when he said:

> Philippians 4:11
> "11 Not that I speak in respect of want for I have learned, in whatsoever state I am, therewith to be content".

This comment does not speak of lack, but rather that Paul knew God provided for every need, no matter what situation in life, he might find himself. Paul determined, no matter what, he would be content.

Reflection Time:

Only Luke records this miracle, and looking at the purpose of that gospel, we see that Luke wrote it clearly to show *the humanity of Yeshua.* It is important that believers understand Yeshua was both fully God *and fully human,* His humanity expressed wonderfully in many ways, including that of a servant to God and others. That *servant-like attitude* comes clear throughout Luke's gospel, reflecting what the book of Isaiah said about the Messiah:

Isaiah 42:1

"1 Behold my servant whom I uphold; mine elect in whom my soul delighteth; I have put my spirit upon him: he shall bring forth judgment to the Gentiles."

Isaiah 52:13

13 Behold my servant shall deal prudently;
he shall be exalted and extolled and be very high.

One might wonder why Luke thought it so important to record this miracle, which the other gospels left out. Does this miracle reflect servanthood? You might like to reflect upon this, and as you do, consider the following as a possibility.

In ancient times, the first-born son was a very important part of any family. If the son followed biblical protocol, he had an enormous responsibility as he grew up. He would help with the family, serving them in a selfless way to assist in the provision and care of the family. In the parents' later years, the oldest son naturally took care of them, if they could no longer handle their own care, hence the reason for giving the first son a double portion of the inheritance.

Now, Yeshua was the Oldest Son, and of course, it goes without saying that, after the death of Joseph, He took up the responsibility to care for His mother, brothers, and sisters. By the time this miracle took place, Yeshua had entered His ministry, but He still saw to His earthly family's care, whenever needed. We see this by looking at the words of Yeshua from the cross when He asked the Apostle John to care for His mother,

> John 19:26-27
> "26 When Yeshua therefore saw his mother, and the disciple standing by, whom he loved, he saith unto his mother, Woman, behold thy son! 27 Then saith he to the disciple, Behold thy mother! And from that hour that disciple took her unto his own home."

It is obvious then, that Yeshua still held a watchful eye over His earthly family. Yeshua, however, trusted His Heavenly Father for all their provisions, no matter the situation. This same skill, which comes by faith and trust in God, His disciples must learn as well.

When Yeshua sent His call to Peter and others to follow Him, in this case James and John, the sons of Zebedee, scripture records that they forsook all and followed Him. "Forsaking all" here pertained to their fishing business, *not their family responsibilities.* Peter was a married mankind. We find that in the scripture, at a time when Yeshua visited Peter's house:

> Matthew 8:14
> "14 And when Yeshua was come into Peter's house, he saw his wife's mother laid, and sick of a fever."

Yeshua never expected His followers to abandon the care of their families, however, He showed them that the Lord would provide, supernaturally, if necessary, for their family's needs. This lesson on Lake Kinneret, which shows God's sovereignty over nature, gave the disciples much food for thought regarding God's abilities. Additionally, the practicality of that miracle providing the needed income for their families, made it possible for these disciples to walk daily with Yeshua, learn the many things Yeshua taught them, and thus, be the equipped vessels Yeshua commissioned to carry the message of salvation, after His resurrection and ascension.

Dear Reader, you may have many other thoughts as to why the Apostle Luke saw it necessary to speak about this miracle, so please take some time and investigate your personal thoughts further. As you think about these things, as well as God's power over nature, consider asking yourself if you know God in the way Jeremiah declared Him:

Jeremiah 32: 27
    27 Behold, I am YeHoVaH, the God of all flesh: is there anything too hard for me?

CANDIDATE FOR A MIRACLE

COURSE 305

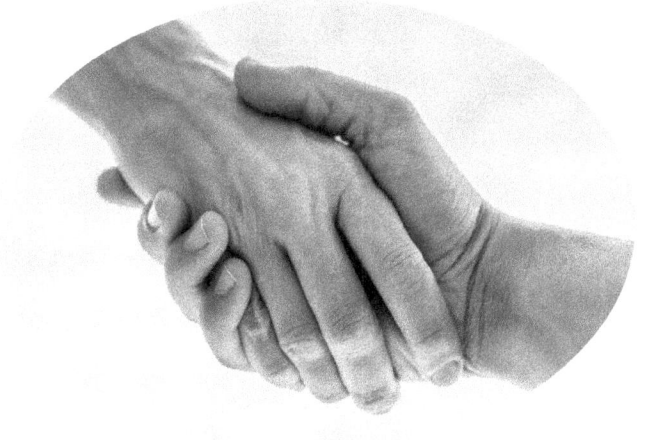

SECTION 2

RECEIVING THE MIRACLE
(continued)

In receiving your miracle
Recognize God's Presence

And the same day, when the even was come, he saith unto them, Let us pass over unto the other side. 36 And when they had sent away the multitude, they took him even as he was in the ship. And there were also with him other little ships. thirty-seven And there arose a great storm of wind, and the waves beat into the ship, so that it was now full. 38 And he was in the hinder part of the ship, asleep on a pillow: and they awake him, and say unto him, Master, carest thou not that we perish? 39 And he arose, and rebuked the wind, and said unto the sea, Peace, be still. And the wind ceased, and there was a great calm. 40 And he said unto them, Why are ye so fearful? how is it that ye have no faith? 41 And they feared exceedingly, and said one to another, What manner of mankind is this, that even the wind and the sea obey him?

Mark 4:35-41

Three gospels record this miracle:

Matthew	Mark	Luke
8:23-27	4:35-41	8:22-25

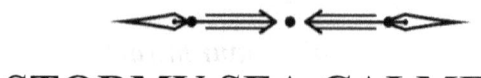

STORMY SEA CALMED

BACKGROUND SETTING
One evening, at the command of Yeshua, He and His disciples entered a ship and set sail for the other side of Lake Kinneret (the Sea of Galilee). Yeshua, weary after a long day, fell fast asleep in the back of the ship. As He slept, suddenly a great wind arose, causing gigantic waves to batter that little ship sailing in the lake. Fearing for their lives, the disciples felt they had no recourse but to awaken Yeshua, exclaiming they were all about to die. Rising from sleep, Yeshua rebuked the wind and calmed the lake, saying, "Peace, be still". Immediately, the wind and water obeyed.

OPERATIVE MINDSETS
As seasoned fishermen, these sailors knew well the Lake, including its reputation for sudden storms. Most likely, as any fisherman battles the raging sea, the disciples struggled to keep the ship afloat, perhaps even bailing out water washed in from the angry

waters. By the time they decided to awaken Yeshua, their words reveal their mindset, "Master, do you not care that we perish?"[59] Death, to their mind, was inevitable, as the angry lake left no other alternative.

MIRACLE PLATFORM

Today, as any ship enters waters, there are standard procedures to ensure safety. All possible preparations are made not to leave survivors abandoned at sea. Life vests are ample in number, normally one for every passenger. Larger ships, such as ocean liners or ferries, have ample life rafts, fitted with special supplies such as food, water, special emergency health aids, as well as equipment to signal other ships for help.

That luxury was not enjoyed by the fishermen of Yeshua's day.[60] Any ship caught in a violent storm, where waves filled up their tiny craft, meant certain death by drowning for those on board. As the ship went up and down, to and fro, tossed by the wild waves of the sea, we see here a clear picture of the need for this miracle, but what was its platform?

Its platform came as the disciples awakened that special passenger on board. They had been with Him

---

[59] Mark 4:39 b

[60] If you go to Israel today, you can actually see the same type of craft used by the Disciples. They have a website with a picture of the ship at www.Yeshuaboat.com.

long enough to know that He had His ways with the Almighty. Surely, He knew how to rescue them from this situation, which was way out of the hands of any human being to resolve! Surely, He must do something or else they would all drown!

REVELATION OF GOD

Experienced fishermen, familiar with Lake Kinneret knew that unless God's hand intervened, they would all die. Perhaps, they expected Yeshua to pray and ask God to save them. After all, He was a holy mankind and they sinners! Perhaps they thought His chances of persuading God to act on their behalf was better than theirs.

Their thoughts are not revealed to us, only their astonishment as they saw Yeshua arise, then speak to the wind and sea, and watch the response of these powerful forces of nature as they obeyed Him. With the quieting of the wind and waters, they received a revelation of the Almighty One operating through the voice of the Son of Man in their midst. Indeed, this person standing in their midst differed from every other person they knew yet paralleled the greater prophets such as Moses who had led the children of Israel through the Red Sea. This mankind, this Yeshua, harnessed both wind and waves with but a Word. *What kind of a mankind was this?* [61]

---

[61] Mark 4:41 paraphrased.

This revelation of power, shown amid their troubles as He rose to rebuke the wind and calm the sea, shows the God of Israel ready, willing, and able to reach out and help His Own. It demonstrates His power as far greater than the forces of nature. This simple word spoken by Yeshua echoed from the platform of their emergency need, to bring forth this mighty miracle.

A FEW MORE INSIGHTS

Earlier, Yeshua told the disciples that they were going to the other side of the Lake. Hopes of reaching the other side of the sea took a dive into despair amidst the noise and force of the gale winds blowing against the tiny ship. Yeshua utterance "to go to the other side" lay buried, forgotten in the middle of their struggle for survival. Often, that is just the case, whenever human beings find themselves in situations of grave danger. It seems the harsh reality of the moment overpowers the normal calm in which a person lives and promises of God not yet realized, seem impossible.

Suddenly, when all is out of control, when everything available to human beings proves inadequate, and death stares us square in the face, hope can easily flee away. Hope, in fact, did vanish after all their efforts to stabilize their ship failed. With death by drowning staring them in the face, they felt powerless and at the mercy of mighty storm threatening to take their lives.

While the record of the event in Mark does not tell us about the other ships, we can conclude, if they were nearby, no help from them was expected, nor received. Rescue ships, therefore, were not an option. Panic stricken, they awakened Yeshua as He slept in the back part, (the stern) of the ship.

"Don't you care that we are all going to die?" was their greeting to Yeshua. In those words, we hear problems of what lay inside the heart of the disciples. Surely, the tossing back and forth in the waters of Lake Kinneret; the howling of the wind; the noise of the disciples' battling for their lives should have been enough atmosphere to wake up Yeshua. Yet, He did not stir. Was He ignoring their plight? Will He sleep while they all drown?

Upon awakening, assessing the situation quickly, Yeshua rebukes the wind, and speaks to the sea. With the utterance of His Words, everything became calm. Yeshua, sound asleep in the tiny sea craft, nevertheless, was their solution. *God, in their midst, was mighty*!

Zephaniah 3:17
> 17 The LORD thy God in the midst of thee is mighty; he will save, he will rejoice over thee with joy; he will rest in his love, he will joy over thee with singing.

How easily, but understandably, the disciples forgot the Word of Yeshua declaring they would *go to the other side of the lake.* Later, in their lives, they would learn to trust His Words, but in this incident filled with terror, they were not ready to enter that state of trust. They were not yet ready to stake their lives on the character of the One Who called them!

As we look on this miracle, we must remember that Yeshua's life spelled out to the disciples the image of the Father, the One true God. After knowing Yeshua for a season, they saw the truth about the Father, for this is Who Yeshua came to show the world.

God's true image, shown through mankind's behaviour, had been lost. Who knew Him as He was: kind, merciful, full of compassion and love? Few indeed, therefore, saw this picture of God, although well shown in the Hebraic scriptures, this image of God needed to come to the front. Exposure to religious rhetoric, routine practices, and traditions by-passed, even hid that revelation of God.

These disciples, however, and every disciple of Messiah, must learn to move past the outer courts of religious experiences and its practices. They must settle into the holy place where they truly know, personally, the character, nature and power of the God of Abraham, Isaac, and Jacob, Who walks with them, in every aspect of life.

MIRACLE SPECIFICS

Thus far, we discussed the various elements of this incident: *the ship, the wind, the rising waves, and fear of death.* We also looked at how God resolved this situation, namely through Yeshua, but we still have a few things yet to consider. One thing is the source of the storm.

Many scholars believe on that specific day at sea the storm's root originated in ha satan, (the adversary) who tried, in one felled swoop, to wipe out the entire future plan of God by eliminating Yeshua as well as His Disciples. That possibility may well exist, but God's plans are always greater and go far deeper than the adversary of humankind realizes. If ha satan caused the wind and the raging sea, how easily his plans were defeated with the word[62] from the Master, Yeshua! No matter the source of the storm, however, Yeshua's words ended it, producing a calm, which returned the Lake and its surroundings back to normal.

After the scene became calm, something rather astounding comes forth in the disciples' words, "What manner of mankind is this, that even the wind and the sea obey him?"[63] These first six words, "What manner of mankind is this?" gives us a clear indication of their recognition of Yeshua's humanity, serving mankind in their time of need.[64]

---

[62] Yeshua, of course, is the Word of God
[63] Mark 4: 41
[64] Showing Yeshua as a Servant is the theme of Mark's gospel

Their last nine words, *"that even the wind and the sea obey him"*, shows their acknowledgement of Yeshua's qualities like none other. Certainly, this mankind was unlike any other. While, at this point, they may not know His deity, they surely knew of His human qualities of love and compassion, which also set Him apart from any other person, even far above the prophets, about which their faith spoke. Indeed, God was with this mankind, and later they would fully understand Yeshua was God in the flesh.

A SURFACE MEANING

This Teacher, Yeshua, who taught His Disciples, certainly had their attention. In looking at this miracle, the disciples saw greatness in Yeshua, as they marked well His power over nature. Earlier in the time spent with Yeshua, they saw **His faith** in God to provide for them, but this experience on Lake Kinneret went past the daily needs of life.

This event elevated the minds of the disciples and raised their thinking well past their original concept of possibilities. Their thinking must shift to a different place to break the mould of their perception of God and His Messiah. They must truly grasp God's character, realizing not just His power over nature, but His desire to see them rescued from this particular situation.

Additionally, Yeshua asleep in the ship's stern shows a powerful picture of God in their midst. While God never sleeps, the fact of Yeshua's availability reminds us that God is as close as the mention of His name! His presence is real, for none came flee away from it!

Psalm 139:11-13

> "11 If I say, Surely the darkness shall cover me; even the night shall be light about me. 12 Yea, the darkness hideth not from thee; but the night shineth as the day: the darkness and the light *are* both alike *to thee*. 13 For thou hast possessed my reins: thou hast covered me in my mother's womb".

Even in the midst of this tempest wind and raging sea, God's Presence meant their survival. God re-enforced this lesson, which went deeper than any verbal teaching. It pointed to a need for them to put ***their faith*** into practice in a way to alter circumstances far beyond the control of mankind. Since God is with you, nothing is impossible! Therefore, we have Yeshua's question ringing loud and clear when He said, "Why are ye so fearful? How is it that ye have no faith?" [65] If the disciples actively ignited their faith knowing God's Presence remained with them, they would see the other side of the seashore. No need for fear!

---

[65] Mark 4:40

Fear, which seemed so natural to those in that tiny ship on the Lake, *has no place in a life of faith*. Fear and faith are opposites, just like the north and south pole. If one has faith, they cannot operate in fear. Fear, if allowed to rule, robs a person of their opportunity to trust in God, and thus blinds them to see that needed platform for their miracle.

Fear paralyzes or freezes the mind, while faith positions the person to reach beyond the immediate situation to call upon God, knowing somehow, someway, He will respond. With faith, a person trusts in God's abilities; trusts in the fulfilment of His commitment to His own; and trusts in His Faithfulness.

In other words, faith focuses not on self, nor humans nor their amazing abilities to resolve certain matters, but faith, rather, rests on God, and on God alone. Faith, not fear, must take charge of the situation, and elevate it to God for His Hand in the matter.

Psalm 115:11
   11 Ye that fear YeHoVaH, trust in YeHoVaH: he is their help and their shield.

Proverbs 3: 5
   5 Trust in YeHoVaH with all thine heart; and lean not unto thine own understanding.

A DEEPER MEANING

Every miracle performed by Yeshua met a need, but in all things, Yeshua never desired people to focus on the sign or wonder. He wanted humankind to look at God, and to recognize why He came as God's Messiah: *to save humankind from their sins.* Salvation, in God's eyes, is the highest goal. Signs and wonders without salvation, still leave humankind eternally lost. Eternity is a long time.

Our lifetime, here and now, really pales when compared to the length of eternity. Thus, signs and wonders, while given of God to help us see His greatness, are not the focus. They are things of the moment of this earth which pass away[66], however, one who is born of God's Spirit, becomes a new creation, an eternal being. Looking then, to the deeper meaning of the miracle, let's look a bit more at Yeshua. Yeshua is God's Messiah and as the Apostle John records, He is the Word of God.

John 1:14
> 14 And the Word was made flesh, and dwelt among us, (and we beheld his glory, the glory as of the only begotten of the Father,) full of grace and truth.

---

[66] This is not to say that signs and wonders are not important. They are part of spreading the gospel, however, the focus should be on the gospel, not on the signs and wonders.

Since Yeshua is the Word of God, we need to look at the words He spoke in this miracle. Let's begin by the first words of Yeshua that Mark records:

Mark 4: 35 b
> 35 b *"he said unto them, Let us pass over unto the other side."*

At first, one might think this is simply directions given to the disciples. Surely, they thought the same thing, however, when God speaks, every word spoken carries with it certain properties.

Isaiah 55:10
> 10 For as the rain cometh down, and the snow from heaven, and returneth not thither, but watereth the earth, and maketh it bring forth and bud, that it may give seed to the sower, and bread to the eater: 11 So shall my word be that goeth forth out of my mouth: it shall not return unto me void, but it shall accomplish that which I please, and it shall prosper in the thing whereto I sent it.

Here the prophet Isaiah compares the Words out of God's mouth to the Godly purpose of rain. Rain falls from the heaven, and so does snow. They do not go back up into heaven again in the same manner as they come down. Rain and snow water the earth. The earth profits from their affect as things planted upon the earth live, producing fruitfulness. That fruitfulness eventually feeds mankind and thus sustains him.

In Isaiah's comparison, he mentions seed for the sower, and bread to the eater. Just as the rain and snow have a purpose, and fulfilling that purpose brings forth and sustains life, so does the Word of God. It never comes back with its assignment unfulfilled. God's Word always completes its purpose, doing exactly as God intended as He spoke those words.

Reflecting upon the words Yeshua spoke to His disciples, we see that He declared, "Let us pass over to the other side". These words meant that all life on board that tiny craft sailing in the Lake of Kinneret *will arrive* on the other side of the Lake.

Yeshua's words to Yeshua's disciples in the past, words such as these seemingly instructional words, held only a surface meaning, but once they understood this Teacher was the Son of God, the actual Word of God, His words must move past their face value. This lesson the disciples had not yet learned, but soon they would remember the experiences they had with Him, as well as His instructional teachings.

In days to come, Yeshua uttered a commission, after His resurrection and prior to His Ascension. This took them places, many of which were difficult. No matter the place, no matter the situation, no matter the other times when danger threatened their lives, they could count on His Faithfulness, His ability to resolve situations.

In the tiny craft, Yeshua rested, trusting His Father, no matter what. When the time came for the disciples to experience life without Yeshua's physical presence with them, they could rest in Yeshua's omnipresence, in the person of God Almighty. Knowing Yeshua, seeing the Father in Him, they could rest in God's Presence with them at all times. His strength, His power, might, or whatever the situation needed, awaited the release of their faith. Just call on God! He is in their midst. He is mighty and He will see them through to the other side of each circumstance they faced.

Even though, in that time coming, these disciples could no longer reach out and touch Yeshua, as they did in that tiny craft amidst the storm at sea, they could remember and trust His Words, *"I am with you always, even unto the end of the world."*[67] His Presence, ever before them, showed His great love for them. Only, a prayer away, for the one who learns to trust God for His purposes to culminate.

---

[67] From Matthew 28:20 b

Faith in Yeshua, Who came to bring all humanity to the Father, should produce, first hand, exactly as the Psalmist wrote:

> Psalm 46: 1-3
> 1 God is our refuge and strength, a very present help in trouble. 2 Therefore will not we fear, though the earth be removed, and though the mountains be carried into the midst of the sea; 3 Though the waters thereof roar and be troubled, though the mountains shake with the swelling thereof. Selah.

MINDSETS CHALLENGED

When death stares people straight in the face they react, often with fear. That's why soldiers are trained for battle. Their former life's experiences often dictate undesirable responses for the soldier in battle, and so, each soldier receives intense training, with its repeated drills, which enforce a behavioural response that the army expects to function in battle.

That training, reinforced repeatedly, is set to trigger proper militant reactions, when needed in battle. Thus, the soldier functions in harmony with his unit. Together, functioning in one direction, they work as a team to obtain the objective set by the commanding officers. They are trained to face fear, overcome it, not be ruled by it.

Keeping that same thought in mind, realize that circumstances in every believer's life are potential trainers. Some reactions are undesirable, causing ungodly responses, while others are positive, causing God-like responses. What determines the response *partly* depends on how they have been programmed prior.

Looking back into the story of the disciples in the craft on the Lake Kinneret, we see a perfectly normal response to a threatening situation: *fear*. Fear, itself, is not a negative, as often it causes adrenaline to race through the body, enabling strength to escape dangerous situations. Fear, however, can overshadow a person's thinking abilities, paralyzing them from doing anything. That helpless state is never to be the lot for believers.

Repeatedly, in scripture, believers are told not to be afraid. Situations of fear do arise, but when fear pokes its head, faith needs to take a front seat. That lesson is a primary part of the "believer's training", beginning from the first time they face fear, moving onward to every situation they encounter, which gives occasion for fear to arise. If, whenever fear pokes its ugly head, faith arises instead, believers move ahead with God, thus facing fear and its limitations. Consequently, faith's lesson speaks as it takes the believer past fear's restraint.

Faith training, like that of a soldier's drill, comes to the front, as believers learn to establish a life of faith. That lifestyle, however, requires a change of mindset, a change of reaction whenever in difficult situations. Thus, the Lord allows situations to touch His children's life that *require faith's response*. If one looks on every such situation as training, even in the small things, then when the bigger challenges appear, training helps to erect faith and push away fear.

Faith unlocks the frozen mind that cannot think and focuses on God, Who has the answer. A believers training by God, intends to reinforce faith as a responding reaction, and that happens when mindsets are pliable and aligned with God's Word and His principles.

Along those same lines of changing mindsets, believers must learn to grasp the difference between God's Word and that of a human being. A friend, a parent, or another trusted source, when speaking in sincerity, mean every word they say. As far as it is possible with them, their integrity ensures they keep their word.

At times, certain events take place which make it impossible for a person of integrity to see their word come to pass, simply because they are human and subject to such things which are beyond their control. ***That never happens with God!*** Nothing is beyond the control of the Almighty One! So, not only does God always remain in control, but looking at His Word, *(Isaiah 55:10-11, as quoted earlier in this chapter)*, we see that God's Word never fails in its purpose.

Yeshua said, *"Let us pass over to the other side"*. As He said that, His Word, divine in origin and power, went forth in total faith, to open the passageway to the other side. His Words, establish a pathway for the specific action to follow. No matter the circumstances arising against His Word, things such as wind and a stormy sea, could not stop that which was already established: *the pathway to cross over to the other side.*

This lesson, His Disciples had yet to learn, and quite frankly, so do we! There are properties that make God's Word different to the word of humankind. We may mean what we say and have the best intentions and personal integrity to keep our word, however, things do arise which cause the words to ring hollow and empty. God, however, *not only means the Word, but the instant it manifests, it establishes God's intentions. No part of God's Word returns to Him empty!*

For believers (as well as all humankind), this is another challenging mindset. We are conditioned, by living upon this earth, with circumstances where words are conversation or communication and can seem fruitless. When looking at God's Word, we must learn to think outside of the box, to recognize that God's Words are more than mere verbal communication. Yeshua, in speaking about His own words, said this:

John 6:63
> 63 It is the spirit that quickeneth; the flesh profiteth nothing: the words that I speak unto you, they are spirit, and they are life.

This sounds like the words of Solomon when he spoke of God's Words:

Proverbs 4:20-22
> 20 ¶ My son, attend to my words; incline thine ear unto my sayings. 21 Let them not depart from thine eyes; keep them in the midst of thine heart. 22 For they are life unto those that find them, and health to all their flesh.

A FEW ADDED THOUGHTS
When one walks with God upon a journey, such as the disciples did with Yeshua, there must come a realization of trust in that relationship. Trust in God's goals as being best for all; trust in God's intentions as being honourable and profitable for His Kingdom and therefore for us; trust in His Words, knowing they are without deceit, trickery, or emptiness.

We must learn to change all our mindsets that speak contrary to the Word of God! It must be with us, as it was with the Psalmist who wrote this:

Psalm 12: 6
> 6 The words of YeHoVaH are pure words: as silver tried in a furnace of earth, purified seven times. 7 Thou shalt keep them, O LORD, thou shalt preserve them from this generation for ever.

Every day, believers face situations, some of them, potential for fear's entrance. In all the situations, which may even seem small and petty, let us learn to walk by faith, whether fear wants to poke its head or not. Let us learn to live out our lives walking by faith, trusting the Lord beyond what our eyes see, our ears hear, or our heart perceives.

Dear reader, let us present each situation in our life, big or small, before God. There, let us learn to respond in that situation the way that God desires. As we do this with everything, we train for those more challenging encounters in life. We train ourselves to take hold with the eye of faith on the prize, remembering God's Presence, which never departs from us. We might not feel His Presence. We might not see evidence of His Presence, immediately, but our faith holds on to its reality!

Whatsoever stands in front of us, *(or behind, beside, above or beneath)*, whether day or night, becomes an impetus to shift our mindset away from fear to stand with the mindset of faith. Let us remember that God's

Presence never departs from our midst, and He is mighty! As we push forward in faith, we fulfil another scripture statement, which appears four times in 4 different books of the Bible:

Habakkuk 2:4
> 4 Behold, his soul which is lifted up is not upright in him: but *the just shall live by his faith*.

Romans 1:17
> 17 For therein is the righteousness of God revealed from faith to faith: as it is written, *The just shall live by faith*.

Galatians 3:11
> 11 But that no mankind is justified by the law in the sight of God, it is evident: for, *The just shall live by faith*

Hebrews 10:38:
> 38 *Now the just shall live by faith*: but if any mankind draw back, my soul shall have no pleasure in him.

Reflection Time:

In this miracle of the stormy sea calmed, God, once again, used something the disciples had within their grasp. First, He used the words of Yeshua, which teaches us that in every situation we can *look for His Words, His Promises* to see us through. Next, He used the *Presence of Yeshua in their midst.* Thus, we remember that Yeshua is with us and, since that is true, nothing with God is impossible.

Dear Reader, how do you handle situations in your everyday life: *by faith, by fear, or by handling it all on you own?* If you have not yet learned to live your life by faith, there is no time like the present to allow the Lord to begin training you to respond in faith to all circumstances that knock on your door throughout of the days of your life. As these kinds of lessons occur, ask the Lord to help you perceive Him, His ability and willingness to help you, as the Bible describes, "an ever-present help in time of need",[68] and how to present it to Him as a platform for a miracle.

---

[68] Psalm 46:1

Beloved child of God, as a believer, you are privileged to know the deep reality of God as He stands by your side, in all circumstances. Even if a believer, through God's leading or life's circumstances, finds themselves face to face with trauma, or even death, they can face things in absolute peace, for they are accompanied by the One Who never leaves them nor forsakes them.[69] You can always trust God's Word, believe His promises, and lean upon Him to bring you the best solution possible for that situation! He is God and nothing catches Him off guard!

A LITTLE MORE THOUGHT

As shown on the opening page of this chapter, three out of four gospels recorded this miracle: Matthew, Mark, and Luke. John's gospel, written to show Yeshua as the Son of God, did not record this miracle. Have you ever wondered why?

Perhaps it is because believers are human and never become deity, however, we can, like Yeshua, rise up in faith and trust God to bring us over to the other side of our problem, no matter the winds blowing against us. Yes, that stormy sea may be something well out of mankind's control and a normal response to that situation is fear, but Yeshua has shown us that we can respond differently.

---

[69] Hebrews 13:5

Believers, today, do not have the privilege of the physical being of Yeshua walking with us, as those disciples had, but we have the Holy Spirit with us. His ability to calm the waters and rebuke the wind is just as real and powerful today as it was back in the days Yeshua walked the earth.

We must always remember that when our humanity fails us, pulls us off course or places us somewhere well past our comfort zone, we have the ever-present One with us, Who understands our humanity. Remembering lessons on His Presence, we confidently trust Him. He stands there, with arms wide open, to embrace us and bring us forward to face situations using His Faith, His Strength, and His Overcoming Power.

Yeshua understands our humanity! He awaits to help us, to position us where we can receive the best from God. We need only call upon Him and activate our trust in Him. Let us therefore, remember, and practice the fact that He is with us, always, in our midst. As such He is mighty!

In receiving your miracle
Recognize God's Faithfulness

And when the day was now far spent, his disciples came unto him, and said, This is a desert place, and now the time [is]⁷⁰ far passed: 36 Send them away, that they may go into the country round about, and into the villages, and buy themselves bread: for they have nothing to eat. thirty-seven He answered and said unto them, Give ye them to eat. And they say unto him, Shall we go and buy two hundred pennyworth of bread, and give them to eat? 38 He saith unto them, How many loaves have ye? go and see. And when they knew, they say, Five, and two fishes. 39 And he commanded them to make all sit down by companies upon the green grass. 40 And they sat down in ranks, by hundreds, and by fifties. 41 And when he had taken the five loaves and the two fishes, he looked up to heaven, and blessed, and break the loaves, and gave [them] to his disciples to set

---

⁷⁰ Brackets indicate words KJV inserted but are not in the original text.

before them; and the two fishes divided he among them all. 42 And they did all eat and were filled. 43 And they took up twelve baskets full of the fragments, and of the fishes. 44 And they that did eat of the loaves were about five thousand men."

Mark 6:35-44

All four gospels record this miracle:

Matthew	Mark	Luke	John
14:13-21	Above	9:12-17	6: 1-15

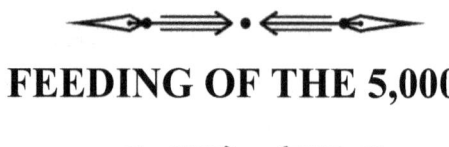

FEEDING OF THE 5,000

BACKGROUND SETTING

Previous verses in Mark's gospel tell us some interesting things about what happened prior to this miracle. Earlier, Yeshua brought His disciples to a quiet place, by ship, to rest and to eat. Onlookers saw them leave by entering the ship. Perceiving their destination, they ran, *on foot*, to meet up with Yeshua. Thus, when He saw them gathered to hear Him, He had much compassion on them and so, He began to teach them many things. [71]

---

[71] Mark 6:30-34

As time went on, Yeshua's disciples thought the crowds, which numbered 5000 men plus women and children, should disperse and go to a place where they might buy themselves some food, for soon the daylight hours would give way to evening. Yeshua had a different idea! "You feed them[72]". What a surprise it must have been to the disciples to hear that command!

OPERATIVE MINDSETS

Their immediate response was common to our human thinking: *do we have enough money to buy what we need*. Yeshua had another idea. In His normal manner, He asked them what they had available. We can tell by their response they had already eliminated that option. They told Yeshua their entire food inventory, including that which the crowd possessed, which totalled five loaves of bread and two fishes[73].

In this desert place, then, where no grocery suppliers set up their markets, Yeshua commanded the crowds to sit down in an orderly manner for easy distribution of the food. They broke into companies of fifties, and hundreds. This crowd size would make it easier to distribute food.

---

[72] Mark 6:37 paraphrased.
[73] Some commentaries believe the fish they had on hand were sardines from the Sea of Galilee. That means these fish were on the tiny size.

MIRACLE PLATFORM

Yeshua's disciples, in obedience to His command, sat down the 5000 men, plus women and children, breaking them into companies of 50 or 100. These hungry people *expected* to eat, due to the words of Yeshua. Most probably wondered how this could be done. After all, in a desert area supplies of food for 5,000 plus people do not exist. Yeshua's faith, the disciples' obedience and the people's expectation, all formed part of the stage set for the miracle.

REVELATION OF GOD

Breaking up into small companies of 50 and 100 made feeding this crowd easier. It also resolved a possible problem where, the stronger and bolder members of the crowd, may push forward to ensure they were fed, first. In a crowd that large, that would cause a problem! Here, we see God's order, then, set up for smooth operation of the task at hand. Yeshua then took what little they had, being the five loaves and two fishes, looked up to heaven, blessed, and broke the loaves. He then gave it to His disciples to give to the people.

In this miracle, we see the face of God's compassion, as well as His Hand of provision, but also His Faithfulness to respond to One Who trusted Him. Yeshua put His faith out there when He told the disciples to feed the crowd, knowing that only God could meet the need. Faithful to respond to Yeshua's faith is important for believers to realize. Since God was faithful to Yeshua's faith, so too will He be faithful to those who are, through faith, in Him!

Thinking about the dynamics of feeding 5000 plus people is definitely a challenging thought, but to do it last minute is unimaginable! Not to mention the cost of such an endeavour! It was just not done! However, the God of all heaven and earth has no limitations in His thinking and last-minute challenges are not last minute to Him! God created the earth, and all in it with just a word, "let there be".

MIRACLE SPECIFICS

Using these few small fish and loaves of bread, God multiplied the available food on hand to satisfy the hunger of the multitude. Yeshua blessed them, and in doing so, extended their limited ability, to satisfy a few, to a virtually unlimited ability to satisfy beyond their natural ability. No one went home hungry! How do we know this, you ask? They had leftovers, enough to fill twelve baskets! This miracle, even momentarily setting aside its powerful message of Yeshua, as the bread of life, shows us the abundance of God and His willingness to provide for mankind, no matter the need!

A SURFACE MEANING

Many of Yeshua's miracles showed God's ability to meet needs. This miracle, in bringing forth a picture of

God as wonderful provider, gained the attention of the crowd, some in a way contrary to God's plans. While many people wondered if Yeshua was a prophet with great power and influence with God, some speculated about Him differently.

Up to the brim with the Roman occupation of Israel, Jews longed for freedom from tyranny. Yeshua's ability to provide gave many listeners ideas to consider Yeshua as their King. Then, with His supernatural ability, they would conquer Rome and be free! In other words, they looked for a type of King David, a warrior as the Messiah. To these people, Yeshua fit the bill.

> John 6:14-15
> 14 Then those men, when they had seen the miracle that Yeshua did, said, This is of a truth that prophet that should come into the world. 15 When Yeshua therefore perceived that they would come and take him by force, to make him a king, he departed again into a mountain himself alone.

This reaction by the crowd was unacceptable in the eyes of Yeshua. He came to save them from slavery and even death, however, His first coming was clearly not the time to crown this rightful King of the universe as such. That crowning cannot take place by the influence and abilities of mankind, rather it will come on the day His Heavenly Father ordained it … at His second coming.

A DEEPER MEANING

We don't have to look too far to discover the deeper meaning of the miracle, for it is recorded in the gospel of John:

> John 6:26-27
> 26 Yeshua answered them and said, Verily, verily, I say unto you, Ye seek me, not because ye saw the miracles, but because ye did eat of the loaves, and were filled. 27 Labour not for the meat which perisheth, but for that meat which endureth unto everlasting life, which the Son of mankind shall give unto you: for him hath God the Father sealed.

Yeshua, in this earlier part of the discourse, pointed out to His listening audience that they must think past their initial mindset of labouring to satisfy the body. Life is more than eating and drinking. There is a far greater need, which is more important since it extends past the parameters of this life and reaches into eternity.

While the body naturally craves food, people must realize that their soul has a hunger, which only the Lord's provision supplies, and in which the soul finds satisfaction. It was important, in thinking of their spiritual wellbeing, they look past the immediate need of their flesh. This would be God's counsel to them!

> Isaiah 25:1
> 1 O LORD, thou *art* my God; I will exalt thee, I will praise thy name; for thou hast done wonderful *things; thy* counsels of old *are* faithfulness *and* truth.

Yeshua, with a focus on their need for everlasting life, invite them to partake of God's full counsel. Unfortunately, that counsel went right over their heads for, in what appears to be an unrelated topic, some in the crowd asked Yeshua how they could do the works of God.

> John 6:28
> 28 ¶ Then said they unto him, What shall we do, that we might work the works of God?

This change of focus seems like a sudden shift away from Yeshua's comments to seek the wellbeing of their soul. Some in the crowd that day were still looking at the natural realm. Their focus shifted past the bottom line of Yeshua's teaching. This question, however, did not take Yeshua off His topic of concern for their eternal destination. So, He returned to His theme of their need for salvation.

John 6:29
> 29 Yeshua answered and said unto them, This is the work of God, that ye believe on him whom he hath sent.

Still, the message puzzled them. They asked Him another question:

John 6:30
> 30 They said therefore unto him, What sign shewest thou then, that we may see, and believe thee? what dost thou work? 31 Our fathers did eat manna in the desert; as it is written, He gave them bread from heaven to eat.

As they continued along the same pathway regarding the carnal or temporal activity of life, Yeshua stayed true to the pathway He needed to present to them. They must learn to look past the surface need of their flesh for their eternal preservation.

John 6:32-40
> 32 Then Yeshua said unto them, Verily, verily, I say unto you, Moses gave you not that bread from heaven; but my Father giveth you the true bread from heaven. 33 For the bread of God is he which cometh down from heaven, and giveth life unto the world. 34 Then said they unto him, Lord, evermore give us this bread. 35 And Yeshua said unto them, I am the bread

of life: he that cometh to me shall never hunger; and he that believeth on me shall never thirst. 36 But I said unto you, That ye also have seen me, and believe not. thirty-seven All that the Father giveth me shall come to me; and him that cometh to me I will in no wise cast out. 38 For I came down from heaven, not to do mine own will, but the will of him that sent me. 39 And this is the Father's will which hath sent me, that of all which he hath given me I should lose nothing but should raise it up again at the last day. 40 And this is the will of him that sent me, that every one which seeth the Son, and believeth on him, may have everlasting life: and I will raise him up at the last day.

Since life does not end at the grave, it becomes imperative that we consider our spiritual need and our future home. God, so faithful to call us to do so, brings forth powerful words from Yeshua's mouth. Words like, "I am the bread of life"; and "He that believes in Me shall never thirst".

Yeshua aimed not to feed them for a day but to give sustenance for their souls. While these words went over their heads, in time, Yeshua knew that many would grasp the meaning and receive Him in the capacity for which He came. How faithful, how merciful of our God to teach us there is more to life than to eat and drink!

MINDSETS CHALLENGED

As one lives upon this earth, we understand provisions are part and parcel for our existence. Without adequate food, shelter, clothing and the like, people die. This miracle, as just mentioned, challenged the participants to look past their flesh needs to that which assures their eternal. This requires a mindset change to think past the survival mode of this earth and grasp the reality of a different kind, one which we need faith to accept its existence.

Yeshua, through feeding 5000+, therefore, challenged the mindset of His listening audience to stretch their thinking beyond what satisfied for their flesh, and even beyond the physical presence of Yeshua they saw in their midst. His Words of instruction, afterward, clearly show that His intent to feed them aimed at reaching His audience then, and in the centuries to come, all who could look past the miracle of loaves and fishes to their spiritual destiny.

To follow Yeshua, one must learn to make their spiritual necessity a priority, *now in this world*, and with the same vigour and urgency as they seek to provide for their physical needs.

A truly redeemed possesses as aspect of Yeshua, which fully satisfies them. That once hungry inner drive longing for something deeper in life no longer exists, for Yeshua satisfies every area. He is indeed our meat and our drink throughout this life!

Dear Reader, as you consider God's counsel and His faithfulness to give it in al circumstances, perhaps take a few moments and think about the questions below.
- do you have that ultimate satisfaction within your relationship with God?
- do you love to feed on the manna from heaven?
- do you recognize God's Faithfulness to you in areas of provision?
- do you consider His counsels of old, (*His Word from both the first and the second Covenant*[74])?

Remember, as you speak to God about these matters that He may well put His finger on something He desires for you to release. If you struggle to do so, please meditate upon His loving care of you. Allow Him to help you walk within His counsels in every area of your life.

---

[74] The Old and New Covenants.

Lean upon His faithfulness to guide you so that you may walk the fullest and most blessed journey possible. Chose to live within His embrace, connecting with Him on every aspect of your being! That experience, while challenging at times, nevertheless, presents the greatest fulfilment on this earth. What an amazing way to live from here to eternity!

9

In receiving your miracle
Recognize God's Awareness

*A*nd when they were come to Capernaum, they that received tribute [money] came to Peter, and said, Doth not your master pay tribute? 25 He saith, Yes. And when he was come into the house, Yeshua prevented him, saying, What thinkest thou, Simon? of whom do the kings of the earth take custom or tribute? of their own children, or of strangers? 26 Peter saith unto him, Of strangers. Yeshua saith unto him, Then are the children free. 27 Notwithstanding, lest we should offend them, go thou to the sea, and cast an hook, and take up the fish that first cometh up; and when thou hast opened his mouth, thou shalt find a piece of money: that take, and give unto them for me and thee.

Matthew 17:24-27

MONEY IN THE FISH'S MOUTH

BACKGROUND SETTING

This record, only Matthew records. Keep in mind, Matthew, originally written in Hebrew, focused on Yeshua as King. In reference, then, to this miracle, we need to remember that Kings and their sons do not pay taxes.[75] Additionally, Rome's own citizens were exempt from paying taxes, but the Jews paid taxes for Rome considered them, "non-citizens". Knowing this information helps us to understand Yeshua's comment, *"What do you think, Simon? of whom do the kings of the earth take custom or tribute? of their own children, or of strangers?* Peter saith unto him, Of strangers. Yeshua saith unto him, "Then are the children free[76]."

---

[75] In 1993, Queen Elizabeth of England volunteered to pay taxes to the United Kingdom. Normally, this is not done as monarchs are exempt, and in ancient times, monarchs collected taxes to build up and operate their realm and its expenditures.
[76] Matthew 17:25 b to 26

OPERATIVE MINDSETS

Every Jewish male, over the age of 20, whether rich or poor, gave ½ shekel in payment of religious taxes, yearly. All collected monies then went into the treasury for care of the Temple. Now, Peter knew that he and Yeshua were fervent worshippers of the Jewish faith, so certainly, he and Yeshua *would pay the temple taxes*. This, however, was not the tax mentioned here, but rather Roman taxes. Aware of the tax required by Rome, as well as the fact of the Jews servitude to Rome, such a tax conversation might go in many directions. Nevertheless, so as not to offend, God provided the payment, *but not in a normal manner*. It came by way of a miracle, something that only God, Himself, could cause.

MIRACLE PLATFORM

We know, from other scriptures, that Yeshua had financial gifts given to Him, which He entrusted to Judas to keep, who distributed it as Yeshua requested. We also know that Judas dipped his hand into the funds and helped himself, to the supply.[77] However, this bill's payment came with a significant lesson for Peter.

---

[77] John 12:6 This he said, not that he cared for the poor; but because he was a thief, and had the bag, and bare what was put therein.

It seems that Yeshua desired to make a powerful statement with the coin in the mouth of the fish. This was another way in which God provided. Peter, by this time in his association with the Master, understood not to question Yeshua's orders. Knowing how to fish, and most likely enjoying that aspect of the assignment, went to the sea as directed, caught the fish, pulled out the coin from the mouth of that fish, and then went and paid the tax for the two of them.

Looking on this situation, today we might not grasp the need in the way Peter and the early church saw it. Nevertheless, the necessity for the tax money existed. Peter, like to so many in ministry today, busied himself with the work of God's kingdom and thus, with limited time available did not have the ready funds to pay the debt. Thus, Peter's present occupation with serving Yeshua, learning about the kingdom of God, and other spiritual things, created a void in the provision of that very important matter. That need, stemming from that situation, created the platform for the miracle.

REVELATION OF GOD

We see Yeshua's understanding of His time, both the political aspects involved as well as the attitudes of the people. Above that, we see God in charge of all creatures, great and small, as well as all circumstances, great and small! Additionally, we see God's awareness of the demands of rulers on their people as well as Peter's concerns about this matter, even though the Bible does not tell us his exact thoughts. We see from this situation, however, Peter's willing obedience brought to pass a wonderful miracle which Peter experienced on that day and could remember for his lifetime.

MIRACLE SPECIFICS
Yeshua's instructions became the specifics for the miracle. To see the tax paid, then, faith must take a step forward and follow in obedience, to the Word of God. While in the days of Jonah, God prepared a big fish to take Jonah safely to land, in this scenario, he prepared a fish, one amongst so many, to contain the coin, and then, specifically, to be caught by Peter.

A SURFACE MEANING
Like other miracles of provision, we see that God delivers when we trust Him, no matter the part He assigns to us so that we can walk towards our miracle! Here, God's specifics made it clear that only God could answer this need. To receive the answer, however, Peter must trust God and position himself to receive!

God, therefore, laid out these specifics to help Peter learn to walk by faith, following God's Word in detail. That obedience in this scenario would receive good fruit: *the coin in the fish's mouth.* Later, Peter, called by

God to a new walk of faith, needed this lesson for the season of his life when he would catch men! [78]

A DEEPER MEANING

When we look at this miracle, while we must realize the importance of recognizing Yeshua as the Messiah or King of Israel. We must also take note that He is God. His deity is crucial in understanding our salvation, and here we see, one more time, His connection with His Father, Who put the steps to the miracle in place.

This miracle shows the awareness of God to resolve a problem, along with the controversy of the day connected with payment of the taxes. Also, we see the Omniscience[79] of God, and the ability of Yeshua to connect with His Father, through the Holy Spirit, to bring this miracle to its full realization[80].

MINDSETS CHALLENGED

Most likely, by this time in walking with Yeshua, His Disciples learned the variety of methods by which God answered their needs. Peter learned that the Master's Ways might be different, but yet they worked! While

---

[78] Matthew 4:19, "And he saith unto them, Follow me, and I will make you fishers of men".

[79] All knowing abilities

[80] On a personal note, I also think it shows the good sense of humour of our Father!

we don't know Peter's mindset, it seems as if his mind began to think differently. In modern terms, Peter needed to learn to think outside the box. He needed to look past the normal aspects of human provision. Learning to expect the unexpected seems to be a key in learning to walk with Yeshua.

We, like Peter, know, from this miracle and others, that our mindset must shift from looking at situational specifics with their limitations, to the unlimited God. He has many great and awesome characteristics, amongst them, the ability to love, care and rule, when necessary, over all creatures, great and small. We see this here, in the example of the fish, called by God to do *its* part in the miracle, obeying the very commands of God.

To see God as unlimited in His ability to help us, we need to remember that God sees every aspect of our life, with every microscopic detail. God's awareness of our need goes far deeper than our awareness! In His infinite wisdom, His Awareness extends into all those detailed places touching our lives. Any one of those details or any place outside of them may well be the place of His answers to our needs.

Candidates for miracles God trains to abandon all restrictions formed by doubt to shift the thinking to envision God as totally aware and totally capable of resolving the problem. Indeed, He is a God without restrictions, without boundaries, and never caught without a plan and purpose!

Can you think, just for a moment, about the thoughts of Peter as he went out to obey the words of Yeshua? Did he think this special assignment fell into the category of a ridiculous assignment. He knew the Master well enough to know it would not be a joke. Perhaps, he wondered why Yeshua would use his experience of fishing, when he laid that aside to follow Yeshua. Perhaps, he doubted along the way. Perhaps not! Maybe he delighted in the excitement of pulling out this fish and seeing the realization of Yeshua's words.

How would you think if that had been you?
As you think about these things, putting yourself into the shoes of Peter, think about the faith element of your own Christian walk. How far are you willing to be stretched in that regard? Or, perhaps, you have been stretched incredibly already and might want to

consider writing down ways in which you held on to your faith, or extended your faith arms to God, or things you did which helped you walk by faith until you reached the other side of that unique challenge.

Allow this wonderful miracle of the coin in the mouth of the fish inspire you remember God's awareness of every detail in your life. Look for His Hand in those details and keep your faith in high gear to receive from him in all those areas. Rest easy, dear one, God's eyes is upon you. His awareness of you and your need motivates Him to move on your behalf. See it and believe it!

> Psalm 139:1-6
> "1 ¶ «To the chief Musician, A Psalm of David.» O LORD, thou hast searched me, and known [me]. 2 Thou knowest[81] my downsitting and mine uprising, thou understandest my thought afar off. 3 Thou compassest my path and my lying down, and art acquainted [with] all my ways. 4 For [there is] not a word in my tongue, [but], lo, O LORD, thou knowest it altogether. 5 Thou hast beset me behind and before and laid thine hand upon me. 6 [Such] knowledge [is] too wonderful for me; it is high, I cannot [attain] unto it."

---

[81] That word in Hebrew means aware!

In receiving your miracle
Recognize God's Dominion

Now in the morning as he returned into the city, he hungered. 19 And when he saw a fig tree in the way, he came to it, and found nothing thereon, but leaves only, and said unto it, Let no fruit grow on thee henceforward for ever. And presently the fig tree withered away. 20 And when the disciples saw [it], they marvelled, saying, How soon is the fig tree withered away! 21 Yeshua answered and said unto them, Verily I say unto you, If ye have faith, and doubt not, ye shall not only do this [which is done] to the fig tree, but also if ye shall say unto this mountain, Be thou removed, and be thou cast into the sea; it shall be done. 22 And all things, whatsoever ye shall ask in prayer, believing, ye shall receive."

Matthew 21:18-22

(Second Account)
"And on the morrow, when they were come from Bethany, he was hungry: 13 And seeing a fig tree afar off having leaves, he came, if haply he might find anything thereon: and when he came to it, he found nothing but leaves; for the time of figs was not [yet]. 14 And Yeshua answered and said unto it, No mankind eat fruit of thee hereafter for ever. And his disciples heard [it]."

Mark 11:12

FIG TREE WITHERS

BACKGROUND SETTING

Walking from Bethany to Jerusalem, about a two-mile walk, Yeshua came upon a fig tree. Most likely He passed by this tree before, but on this day, He stopped to eat from it, however, there He found no fruit.

In accordance with Bible authorities, the time frame of this event was about 4 days before the crucifixion. That means, it was close to springtime, shortly before Passover. At that season, there is a small possibility that some fig trees may have a few leaves on them, but *not fruit*, since it was not the season. Some, who study horticulture, ancient and modern, say, however, a slim possibility existed for some *old fruit* from the last year's harvest to remain on the tree. Most, however, say it is unrealistic for anyone to expect to find fruit on a tree located in such a public place for the many passersby to eat of it. They feel, of a certainty, all its fruit would be gone.

OPERATIVE MINDSETS

Considering the apostles accompanying Yeshua knew the fig tree held no available fruit, it is probable they wondered why Yeshua expected to find figs. If the first action by Yeshua did not surprise them, certainly the second one did. After not finding fig, Yeshua cursed the tree. When it immediately withered, they marvelled.

They questioned Yeshua, Who answered their inquiries by speaking about faith.

Matthew 21:21

> 21 Yeshua answered and said unto them, Verily I say unto you, If ye have faith, and doubt not, ye shall not only do this [which is done] to the fig tree, but also if ye shall say unto this mountain, Be thou removed, and be thou cast into the sea; it shall be done. 22 And all things, whatsoever ye shall ask in prayer, believing, ye shall receive."

To embrace Yeshua's teaching, to move into the realms of greater faith, the apostles required another shift in their thinking. They must think past the two obvious facts in this situation:

1. Why expect fruit from the fig tree not in season?
2. Why speak of faith?

Let's look at it:

1. Why expect fruit from the fig tree?

We know the answer does not rest in the fact of any physical fruit, for Yeshua, if hungered, knew His Father provided food, even if by a miracle. So, why then, did Yeshua go to the fig tree, which was out of season, and expect to eat fruit from it?

In trying to understand this event, some have concluded the answer lies in what the fig tree represented. Some say that representation goes as far back as the garden of Eden. They believe that Adam and Eve clothed themselves with fig leaves after they sinned, [82]therefore, this tree represented the fig free in the garden. Thus, when Yeshua cursed the tree, He showed humankind, for all time, that He'd forever take care of the sin question. Just as the fig tree withered and died, so too sin, in the life of all those who come to Him, withers and die. Admittedly, this is an

---

[82] Genesis 3:7

interesting possibility, however, the Bible does *not say* the tree in the Garden was a fig tree.

What does the Bible say regarding the fig tree?

In Jeremiah 8, YeHoVaH speaks of the time of His visitation to Israel, and to figs as well:

> Jeremiah 8:11-13
> 11 For they have healed the hurt of the daughter of my people slightly, saying, Peace, peace; when there is no peace. 12 Were they ashamed when they had committed abomination? nay, they were not at all ashamed, neither could they blush: therefore, shall they fall among them that fall: in the time of their visitation, they shall be cast down, saith YeHoVaH. 13 I will surely consume them, saith YeHoVaH: there shall be no grapes on the vine, nor figs on the fig tree, and the leaf shall fade; and the things that I have given them shall pass away from them.

A study of this passage shows that its topic makes reference, fugitively to the teachers of Israel, those *without God's heart and understanding of the truth*. These teachers held an ignorance to God's Word, His Torah[83] and His heart, thus, they spoke lies to God's people.

---

[83] This word means instructions of God, not Law as commonly interpreted.

On the day when God visits the people, He shall consume the false prophets and teachers, along with their lies, and thus, in the end, their efforts and their lives, will bear no fruit, *no grapes on the vine, nor figs on the tree.*

2. Why speak of faith?

To understand this question, we first need to understand the overall attitude of the religious leaders in Israel. Through the eyes of scripture, we see that the king, along with his officials, the religious teachers and other spiritual leaders did not understand God's heart, the role of the Messiah, nor the reason why God gave them the Torah.

On that subject Yeshua spoke:

Matthew 5:18
18 For verily I say unto you, Till heaven and earth pass, one jot or one tittle shall in no wise pass from the law, till all be fulfilled.

Yeshua, the Messiah God sent, fulfilled the Torah in every aspect, yet as He stood in front of them, they recognized Him not. In fact, in both passages, prior to the record of this miracle, we read of the triumphant entry of Yeshua into Jerusalem. At that entry, the chief priests and scribes were very displeased.

Matthew 21:14-16
> 14 And the blind and the lame came to him in the temple; and he healed them. 15 And when the chief priests and scribes saw the wonderful things that he did, and the children crying in the temple, and saying, Hosanna to the Son of David; they were sore displeased, 16 And said unto him, Hearest thou what these say? And Jesus saith unto them, Yea; have ye never read, Out of the mouth of babes and sucklings thou hast perfected praise?

Clearly, Yeshua was the Son of God, the Messiah, but the chief priests and scribes did not recognize Him as such. Their teachings, their precepts of the Torah and what it meant, were not in alignment with what God intended. With their teachings, they were blinded, and in their blindness taught others who in turn, shared their blindness.

If one was to receive Yeshua as the Messiah, their mindset must shift from what they were taught by the chief priests and scribes, and read what God, indeed, had intended in the scriptures. Yeshua had come, and He came to fulfil the Torah. He would inaugurate a New Covenant, but that meant that precious, glorious First Covenant, to which the priests and scribes held and wrongly interpreted, must be seen in the light in which God wrote it, not how they interpreted it.

There were clues to that "coming change" for the chief priests and scribes in the Word of God. Of that clue, the Apostle Paul, who had a true revelation of the Messiah, spoke:

Galatians 4:22-31
> 22 For it is written, that Abraham had two sons, the one by a bondmaid, the other by a freewoman. 23 But he who was of the bondwoman was born after the flesh; but he of the freewoman was by promise. 24 Which things are an allegory: for these are the two covenants; the one from the mount Sinai, which gendereth to bondage, which is Agar. 25 For this Agar is mount Sinai in Arabia, and answereth to Jerusalem which now is, and is in bondage with her children.
>
> 26 But Jerusalem which is above is free, which is the mother of us all. 27 For it is written, Rejoice, thou barren that bearest not; break forth and cry, thou that travailest not: for the desolate hath many more children than she which hath an husband. 28 Now we, brethren, as Isaac was, are the children of promise. 29 But as then he that was born after the flesh persecuted him that was born after the Spirit, even so it is now.
>
> 30 Nevertheless what saith the scripture? Cast out the bondwoman and her son: for the son of

the bondwoman shall not be heir with the son of the freewoman. 31 So then, brethren, we are not children of the bondwoman, but of the free.

In simple terms, Paul stated that the two covenants (First and New) are prophetically demonstrated in a type, lived out in the lives of Hagar and Sarah. The son of Hagar (Ishmael), comparatively speaking, is the Torah, (or the First Covenant), and the son of Sarah (Isaac), is the New Covenant. Those of the New Covenant are not the son of the bondwoman, but the son of the free. In other words, believers, in the New Covenant live under Grace and not Torah, for everything under the First Covenant fades in light of the New.

In other words, if you wish to see the Messiah as God designed, then you must look at the Word of God with faith. Look at Yeshua in the First Covenant in the way God presented Him. Don't get caught up in the external trappings of the faith and miss the heart of the matter. Keep that in mind, as you read the following section.

MIRACLE PLATFORM
From the information gathered previously in this chapter, let us conclude that the fig tree, for the sake of this analogy, *represents the Torah*. Paul summed up its purpose:

Galatians 3:24

> 24 Wherefore the law was our schoolmaster to bring us unto Maschiach, that we might be justified by faith.

As a schoolmaster, or teacher, the Torah, as God designed it, existed to lead a person to Messiah. Why? It showed that all humankind are sinners. Once people become convicted of that fact, forgiveness of all their sin lies on the pathway ahead. Knowing Yeshua, the Redeemer of Israel, arrived, receive your salvation, by recognizing role as Messiah, one who paid the punishment for all sin. Once you do that, the door opens wide as God's forgiveness of sins pours over your life.

One platform for a miracle rests in recognizing God's dominion over the requirements for sin's payment. He sets the bar for sin's payment. He hates the ways of mankind that cause one to trust in a religious performance rather than God, Himself.

Looking at this lesson of the fig tree, another platform for a miracle is that of the withered fig tree projecting *an end to spirit of error*. That spirit acts contrary to the Holy Spirit by leading people away from the truth[84].

---

[84] "Howbeit when he, the Spirit of truth, is come, he will guide you into all truth: for he shall not speak of himself; but whatsoever

These two platforms give much room for God to minister to those who cry out for His help.

REVELATION OF GOD

Thinking back to the fig tree, the tree stood along the way from Bethany to Jerusalem, in plain view of passersby. Yeshua hungered and approached it. He knew, both in the natural and in the spiritual, that the fig tree could not give Him fruit because it was not its season. Thinking of the First Covenant, with its hidden revelation, compared to the revelation of Messiah, is like day and night. In the first covenant, without the eyes of faith, it is like living in the dark, in the night. With eyes, however, that now see, it is like living in the light, in the day!

When Yeshua cursed the fig tree, that which was out of season for its fruit, He declared that *the present teachings of Israel's leaders, which did not receive Him, leads to death.* Those teachings, like the fig tree, produce *no fruit*. In other words, Yeshua cursed **the religious system established by mankind, the teachings that did not show the revelation of Yeshua as Messiah.** Teach the First Covenant in that way, and it produces no children. God's children are born of faith!

---

he shall hear, *that* shall he speak, and he will shew you things to come". John 16:13

MIRACLE SPECIFICS

A fig tree, out of season for bearing fruit, was cursed by Yeshua. That tree withered and died and never bore fruit again. Then, Yeshua gave an explanation, which on the surface seems unrelated. Regarding Yeshua's explanation, He spoke of casting a mountain into the sea. Does this connect with the parable of the fig tree?

Consider this:
Wrong doctrines, such as the chief priests, scribes and Pharisees taught, are like mountains of doubt to Yeshua's identity as the Messiah. Speak to that mountain, with faith that Yeshua is the Messiah, and that mountain will get into the sea. "And all things, whatsoever ye shall ask in prayer, believing, ye shall receive".[85]

A new season is upon you, the season for the full revelation of the Torah. That which was hidden in the Torah is revealed. Leave behind that season and enter the new season of revelation of Messiah. There is now a new and better way, a living way to the Father, and that is through Yeshua.

Hebrews 10:14
> 14 For by one offering he hath perfected for ever them that are sanctified. 15 [Whereof] the Holy Ghost also is a witness to us: for after that he

---
[85] Matthew 21:22

had said before, 16 This [is] the covenant that I will make with them after those days, saith the Lord, I will put my laws into their hearts, and in their minds will I write them; 17 And their sins and iniquities will I remember no more. 18 Now where remission of these [is, there is] no more offering for sin. 19 ¶ Having therefore, brethren, boldness to enter into the holiest by the blood of Yeshua, 20 By a new and living way, which he hath consecrated for us, through the veil, that is to say, his flesh; 21 And [having] an high priest over the house of God; 22 Let us draw near with a true heart in full assurance of faith, having our hearts sprinkled from an evil conscience, and our bodies washed with pure water.

Now, with God's Son manifested in the flesh, the New Covenant's inauguration was at hand. Remember, the old season, like the first covenant, no longer plays a role in salvation as it once did in its earlier years. While its principles still teach how to live a holy life before God, as well as teach what displeases God, **the finger it pointed to salvation no longer consists of the sacrifice of bulls and goats!** That season has passed! Now its fulfilment in Yeshua shows points to a new and living way, through *the blood of Yeshua.* Now, this way to eternal life takes it paramount place.

A SURFACE MEANING

Yeshua uttered words and thus, ended the existence of the fig tree. On the surface, we see those words, uttered, in faith, move mountains, or in this case, wither trees. God's judgment of an issue brings the situation to its conclusion. This surface meaning also follows through to a deeper meaning *which is how to speak the words of faith into situations, or how to see situations change by uttering the commands of God, Who has dominion over all things.*

A DEEPER MEANING

In this action of Yeshua, we recognize the power of words. Whether our intentions move in a certain direction or another, words carry an impact as they produce fruit. Which type of fruit they produce depends upon the meaning of the words used. For example, when Yeshua blessed, things had life, when He cursed, they had death. The message of the words, here, demonstrate control of the tongue. Use it for good, but be careful, words can also bring harm.

Going even deeper for meaning, we see in the walk of faith, as we speak God's counsel and use His Words as it is written, it produces fruit.
Speak forth the gospel message and see the realization of a seed of the Word come alive as people are born again and live in Him.

Moving past the utterance of words, we see a oneness necessary of the heart of a believer with the heart of God, so they speak God's very words and see them come to pass. Words like, "rise and be healed" as directed by the Holy Spirit and given in the power of God, produce the fruit of healing. Thus, the relationship with God, walking with Him in the Spirit of Dominion produces great fruit for His kingdom!

In believing on Yeshua, in exercising faith by the power of the Holy Spirit we have a *major ingredient* to moving any mountain! Believe in Yeshua and do the works He did, even greater works because He sits at the Father's right hand. Discard the wisdom given by mankind-made religious teachings and embrace the truth of the Living God!

In looking at the meaning of this miracle, we have one more aspect which some think to be viable, but this author rejects. Let's take a quick look at it.

This miracle, some see as a prophetic picture of Israel cursed by God for rejecting their Messiah. To see this miracle in that light, is to miss the heart of God regarding Israel.

Romans 11:1, 5-8
1 I say then, Hath God cast away his people? God forbid. For I also am an Israelite, of the seed of Abraham, *of* the tribe of Benjamin.

5 Even so then at this present time also there is a remnant according to the election of grace. 6 And if by grace, then *is it* no more of works: otherwise, grace is no more grace. But if *it be* of works, then is it no more grace: otherwise, work is no more work. 7 What then? Israel hath not obtained that which he seeketh for; but the election hath obtained it, and the rest were blinded 8 (According as it is written, God hath given them the spirit of slumber, eyes that they should not see, and ears that they should not hear;) unto this day".

Paul, the Apostle, makes it clear that God did not do away with Israel. In other words, God did not curse

> Symbolically, the fig tree with *no fruit* represents fruitless works, and their *source is the flesh*. External worship, with all its trappings, blind one to the truth, and are often re-enforced by the false teachings, and false prophecies, etc. that interpret the Word of God to be other than what God designed.

Israel for the rejection of Yeshua as Messiah, as some think and teach.

Very simply put, God desires "children", first, to be born of His Spirit, and secondly, to serve Him, not religion.

Any works that produce religion and not true works of God in God's eyes, algin with that fig tree that gave no fruit. God desires an end to such things, but His heart longs for people to repent and come to Him for salvation and forgiveness. Therefore, in this miracle, we see God's mighty provision for salvation for all humankind and His thorough and complete dislike for teachings of mankind which hide the truth!

MINDSETS CHALLENGED
This miracle challenges many mindsets, the bulk of which *remove surface meanings of our faith*. Before going there, let's address one aspect that some people believe and that is that God cursed human beings.

God, on no occasion cursed humankind. Some think He did in the Garden, after sin entered, but reading scripture carefully, we see that is not the case.

1. God cursed *the ground* for mankind's sake.
2. God cursed *the serpent* that allowed itself to be an instrument of the adversary.
3. God, however, *promised humankind* a redeemer and blessed him by removing him from the Garden so he would not eat of the tree of life and be permanently lost! God's goal for humankind has always been an eternity with Him.

To hold such a mindset as to think God cursed humankind, holds to the teachings of humankind.

This mindset, along with others such today's thinking by some Jews, that God wants a revival of animal sacrifices. These mindsets must shift out of the way to embrace the truth of the gospel message.

Truly, New Covenant believers must embrace and live by the fact that Yeshua is Messiah, and with that realization, as we live out our life before the face of God, with God, nothing is impossible. Mountains must move out of the way, including the stumbling stones of doubt and unbelief. Indeed, we must learn to walk by faith, embrace the God of the Impossible and learn to rest in His dominion!

Reflection Time:

Perhaps, dear reader, you might take some time and ask God for His viewpoint on how you live out your faith life before Him. Do you live as Hebrews 10:38 a) declares, or some other way?

Hebrews 10:38 a)

38 Now the just shall live by faith:

In receiving your miracle
Recognize God's Supremacy

And straightway he constrained his disciples to get into the ship, and to go to the other side before unto Bethsaida, while he sent away the people. 46 And when he had sent them away, he departed into a mountain to pray. 47 And when even was come, the ship was in the midst of the sea, and he alone on the land. 48 And he saw them toiling in rowing; for the wind was contrary unto them: and about the fourth watch of the night, he cometh unto them, walking upon the sea, and would have passed by them. 49 But when they saw him walking upon the sea, they supposed it had been a spirit, and cried out: 50 For they all saw him and were troubled. And immediately he talked with them, and saith unto them, Be of good cheer: it is I; be not afraid. 51 And he went up unto them into the ship; and the wind ceased: and they were sore amazed in themselves

beyond measure and wondered. 52 For they considered not [the miracle] of the loaves: for their heart was hardened.

Mark 6:45-52

Add on from John:
Then they willingly received him into the ship: and immediately the ship was at the land whither they went.

John 6: 21

Three gospels record this miracle:

Matthew[86]	Mark	John
14:22-33	above	6:16-21

WALKING ON THE WATER

---

[86] Matthew writes in his gospel the record of Peter walking on the water, sinking, and calling out to Yeshua who immediately saved him. For some additional thought on this subject, be sure to follow up on you own by reading Matthew 14:22-33.

BACKGROUND SETTING

On the Sea of Galilee, (Lake Kinneret) the disciples sailed along, following the instructions of Yeshua. Using this body of water, then, they would travel to Bethsaida and Yeshua would dismiss the crowds and join them later. It is most likely the disciples thought Yeshua, travelling by foot on land, would join them later in Bethsaida. However, this story proved Yeshua had another plan.

OPERATIVE MINDSETS

In looking at the operative mindsets, we see aspects of normal living. As the disciples went towards the ship following Yeshua's orders. Yeshua dismissed the crowds and went up to a high mountain to pray. Once Yeshua finished praying, He looked down upon the Sea of Galilee, (Lake Kinneret). There He saw the disciples toiling, rowing against the wind. According to Mark's record, it was the fourth watch of the night, between 3:00 a.m. and 6:00 a.m. Yeshua began to make His way towards the disciples, not by land, not by boat, but by walking on the water.

In the open sea, the disciples rowed steadily into the contrary wind. Like every sailor wrapped up in the chore of getting to port, their minds fixed tight on their goal. They did not expect the supernatural, but suddenly their natural world underwent an interruption. They see a figure on the water. Perceiving it might be a ghost they cry out in fear.

Unexpectedly, Yeshua's voice breaks through the deafening darkness and the whirling wind, saying, "Be of good cheer: it is I; be not afraid." After identifying Himself, Yeshua came right up to the ship, and with permission by its occupants, He entered it. Immediately, the wind ceased and suddenly the ship was at the other shore. [87]

MIRACLE PLATFORM
Here is yet another time where the Sea of Galilee (Lake Kinneret) is the physical platform for this miracle. On those waters, rowing towards Bethsaida in a contrary wind, the miracles takes place.
   a. Miracle 1: Yeshua walks on water. (Peter joins him, sinks, and then Yeshua rescues him).
   b. Miracle 2: Suddenly, the contrary winds stops and the entire ship with its entire crew end up safely on the other side. (Contrary winds, push you away from your goal, but with Yeshua on board, those contrary winds stopped. All preventing the disciples from fulfilling Yeshua's orders ceased. They stepped out of the boat at their intended destination.)

As Mark's account of this event ends, he tells us that they were amazed beyond measure and wondered. Then, Mark says, they did not consider the miracle of

---

[87] This is from the sister account in John 6:21

the loaves and fishes, because they had hardened hearts.

REVELATION OF GOD

This miracle, if studied entirely from all three gospels, shows three miracles:

1. Yeshua walks on Water
2. Peter walks on Water
3. Immediately, the ship arrives at the other side

God, in preparing the disciples to carry the torch of the gospel, ensured they understood Yeshua was both God and mankind. Many supernatural phenomena were used to reach those disciples, to soften their hearts towards Him. This miracle, in God's eyes, was necessary since the miracle of the loaves and fishes *did not do everything God desired.* In other words, these chosen disciples, the ones in whom Yeshua invested the future, hardened their hearts to receive what God desired they possess for their future role in His kingdom. Thus, to break through, this event occurred.

According to the account in Matthew 14, "Then they that were in the ship came and worshipped him, saying, *Of a truth thou art the Son of God."* This shows us the bottom-line reason for the miracle! Each disciple must understand and receive Yeshua's mandate upon the earth. They must know that He is the Son of God!

This miracle God designed, evidentially, to bring the disciples to this needed conclusion. This is the revelation of God that was necessary, and later put so beautifully into writing by the Apostle John,

John 1:10-14

> 10 He was in the world, and the world was made by him, and the world knew him not. 11 He came unto his own, and his own received him not. 12 But as many as received him, to them gave he power to become the sons of God, even to them that believe on his name: 13 Which were born, not of blood, nor of the will of the flesh, nor of the will of mankind, but of God. 14 And the Word was made flesh, and dwelt among us, (and we beheld his glory, the glory as of the only begotten of the Father,) full of grace and truth.

MIRACLE SPECIFICS

In this miracle, Yeshua showed Himself with supremacy over nature. Even in His earthly state, He had power over the elementary principles of the world, to which all humankind are subject. Suddenly, after His entrance into the ship, the disciples in the ship acclaimed Him as the Son of God, worshipping Him.

Their hearts, *now softened*, meant they fully believed in Him. Next, they are on the other side of the Sea.

Among the prophetic meanings of this miracle, we see an action of God demonstrating what happens when one believes on Yeshua. Scripture says:

> Colossians 1:12-13
> 12 Giving thanks unto the Father, which hath made us meet to be partakers of the inheritance of the saints in light: 13 Who hath delivered us from the power of darkness, and hath translated us into the kingdom of his dear Son:

When one believes in Yeshua, immediately the Holy Spirit does several amazing things, one of which is taking one from beneath the jurisdiction of the power of darkness, translating them into the Kingdom of God. [88]

A SURFACE MEANING

Many people read this miracle and take its meaning as a call for all to live by faith. After all, when Peter tried to walk on the water, but failed, Yeshua said to him, "O thou of little faith, wherefore didst thou doubt?"[89] This is a good surface meaning for, without faith, it is impossible to please God!

---

[88] If you do not understand that principle of salvation, please turn to the Appendix and read, Salvation's Message.
[89] Matthew 14:31

Hebrews 11:6
> 6 But without faith it is impossible to please him: for he that cometh to God must believe that he is, and that he is a rewarder of them that diligently seek him.

A DEEPER MEANING

Faith is a very important part of the life of a believer and must go down deep into their being. The message of this miracle goes deeper. Yeshua is God, Who came in the flesh and walked in the midst of humankind. His work on the cross, which is an awesome miracle in itself, no human being could accomplish on their own. For Yeshua it meant the help of the Holy Spirit both in life, to live a righteous life, and in death, to accomplish the work of the cross.

Hebrews 9:14
> 14 How much more shall the blood of Yeshua Ha' Maschiach, who through the *eternal Spirit*[90] offered himself without spot to God, purge your conscience from dead works to serve the living God?

It is imperative that the first disciples of Yeshua understood His Deity. It is not enough to consider only His humanity, they must come to terms with the fact that He was, is, and always will be, God.

---

[90] The eternal Spirit is another name for the Holy Spirit.

One further deeper meaning shows believers how to respond as they navigate the sea of life, obeying Yeshua's commands. First, believers must remember, the gospel message places them in a ship which moves contrary to the winds of the world. Constantly, darkness presses in around them. So, as they move forward into heaven's assignment, doing the work of the kingdom, it becomes imperative to ensure Yeshua lives in the midst. Then, giving Him the helm, expect Him to bring the deliverers of His heavenly message past the darkness and the world's winds to the arrive in victory on the other side. This happens because believers follow the Son of God, Who is and was and always will be, God Incarnate!

MINDSETS CHALLENGED
John, the Apostle, as shown earlier, fully embraced the idea of Yeshua's deity:

John 1:14
14 And the Word was made flesh, and dwelt among us, (and we beheld his glory, the glory as of the only begotten of the Father,) full of grace and truth.

This shows a change of mindset as the disciples, schooled in Judaism, knew the Shema, which says:

Deuteronomy 6:4
   4 Hear, O Israel: The LORD our God is one LORD:

This, in many ways, if not properly understood, could easily prevent a Jewish person from understanding the Godhead, which includes the Deity of Messiah. When Yeshua walked upon the water, they hailed Him as the Son of God, and after His resurrection, in the sermon preached on the Day of Pentecost, Peter declared Yeshua, the Messiah, the sinless one.

Acts 2:36
   36 Therefore let all the house of Israel know assuredly, that God hath made that same Yeshua, whom ye have crucified, both Lord and Maschiach.

To bring the disciples to this mindset was not an easy task, but miracles, like Yeshua walking on the water, helped them to look past their background teaching, to accept Him as He was. Of course, later, when He opened their minds to the scriptures, they understood in a greater way, but this miracle of walking on water, broke through the ice of their hardened hearts, and challenged their thinking to align them with God's greater plans. How amazing to experience this miracle, declare Yeshua as Lord, and then, suddenly arrive on the shore on the other side of the lake. Indeed, His supremacy governs all circumstances!

Reflection Time:

Many believers learn religious teachings from childhood. Then, one day, just like the disciples in the ship, believers find themselves in an uncomfortable place, which challenges the very foundations of their faith. What happens in the search for truth when the earlier foundation proves misaligned with truth, not entirely based on the whole counsel of God?

Take some time. Seek God. Invite Him into every area of your life, especially the ones you think you can handle on your own. Ask God if you recognize Him supremacy in all things. Ask Him if your life centres around Yeshua. In other words, ask God if Yeshua is in the ship[91]?

---

[91] Remember, if He answers that Yeshua, *at this time*, is not central to your life, a simple prayer of asking forgiveness and for your life to focus on Him, corrects the problem. God never looks to condemn, dear one. He convicts, restores, and brings to a greater freedom in Him.

12

In receiving your miracle
Recognize God's Empowerment

After these things Yeshua shewed himself again to the disciples at the sea of Tiberias[92]; and on this wise shewed he himself. 2 There were together Simon Peter, and Thomas called Didymus, and Nathanael of Cana in Galilee, and the sons of Zebedee, and two other of his disciples. 3 Simon Peter saith unto them, I go a fishing. They say unto him, We also go with thee. They went forth and entered into a ship immediately; and that night they caught nothing. 4 But when the morning was now come, Yeshua stood on the shore: but the disciples knew not that it was Yeshua. 5 Then Yeshua saith unto them, Children, have ye any meat? They answered him, No. 6 And he said unto them, Cast the net on the right side of the ship, and ye shall find. They cast therefore, and now they were not able to draw it for the multitude of fishes. 7 Therefore that disciple whom Yeshua loved saith unto Peter, It is the Lord. Now

---

[92] Another name for the Sea of Galilee

when Simon Peter heard that it was the Lord, he girt [his] fisher's coat [unto him], (for he was naked,) and did cast himself into the sea. 8 And the other disciples came in a little ship; (for they were not far from land, but as it were two hundred cubits,) dragging the net with fishes. 9 As soon then as they were come to land, they saw a fire of coals there, and fish laid thereon, and bread. 10 Yeshua saith unto them, Bring of the fish which ye have now caught. 11 Simon Peter went up, and drew the net to land full of great fishes, an hundred and fifty and three: and for all there were so many, yet was not the net broken."

John 21:1-11:

2nd CATCH OF FISH

BACKGROUND SETTING

John's gospel alone records this miracle. It occurred after Yeshua's resurrection, before His ascension. Simon Peter, Thomas, Nathanael, James and John, the sons of Zebedee, (Simon Peter's fishing partners), and two other disciples were out fishing all night long. This is evidence that they went back to their former occupation before they walked with Yeshua. Unfortunately, their night's effort produced nothing.

In the morning, as they returned to the shore, Yeshua spoke to them, asking them if they caught any fish. No, was their reply. Yeshua told them to cast their net on the right side of the ship for a catch. They did so, and so great was the catch that they could not pull up the net. Immediately, Simon Peter recognized the person could be none other than Yeshua.

Fishermen, at that time, often removed their outer tunic when fishing, and this Peter had done. So excited to know this mankind was Yeshua, he jumped into the waters and made his way to land. The ship and its occupants followed.

From this encounter with Yeshua, especially this one of the second catch of fish, Yeshua both reassured the disciples that death could not hold Him, and empowered them for their future life. That life, as we seen in looking back at their service to Him, entailed a martyr's death for all but John. John, endured great suffering, however, and an exile on a desert island. Each disciple needed the encouragement Yeshua gave them, as He empowered them for their service to God and His kingdom.

OPERATIVE MINDSETS
Messiah's disciples returned to their former way of thinking, back to their daily routine, to take up their previous lifestyle before they met Yeshua. Income to

feed their families, as usual, was obviously the priority at hand. Yet, one more time, in their lives as fishermen they laboured through the night without a catch.

MIRACLE PLATFORM

Here the disciples, at their extremity, tried to move on. Earlier, Yeshua's love, teaching, and effective leadership, touched their lives, but now, after the death, burial, and resurrection of Yeshua, they were left going through the motions of daily life. Thus, they returned to their life and means of providing for their families moving in the way they did prior to meeting Yeshua.

Their hearts, rejoiced at His appearance to them post crucifixion, but the way to pick up the pieces and move on had not yet be revealed to them. Indeed, these disciples were ready to receive a mighty miracle from God.

REVELATION OF GOD

Peter, the group leader, said he was going to go fishing. Likewise, his fellow friends joined him in the same ship. What they expected on that day, we don't know, but how they needed direction from God. Although Yeshua appeared to Peter twice since the resurrection, it seems Peter's leadership of the group did not take shape in any form of following their Master, speaking forth His Message.

Later, after Pentecost, that message would be foremost in Peter's mind, as well as those of the other disciples. Then, they'd have the power, but for now, they were uncertain of their future. How do they process their 3 years with Yeshua? How do they interpret His death, burial, and resurrection in terms of their commitment and service to Him?

As they went about doing what they knew how to do best, fishing, the Lord would appear to them, and He would give them the new direction they so desperately needed, especially Peter. Each appearance since the cross had a specific purpose and a message, and the message written in the miracle, would help them beyond measure.

Easily, the Lord might suddenly appear in their ship, or walk again on the water, but He chose none of those things. He utilized the method by *which He first called Peter:* to provide a large catch of fish for them after their own labours failed to do so.

Yeshua showed Himself as the risen Lord, yes, and more than a Provider, for here, he reached out to them in their wounded condition and met them with great compassion, concern, and love through this miracle of the catch of fish. He was still with them! It wasn't all over! There was a future for them!

MIRACLE SPECIFICS

Near to the shore, and not out in the deep, as the last time, Yeshua told them to cast their net on the right side of the ship. As the fish packed into the nets, the disciples would identify the One on the shore as Yeshua. Then, once on the shore themselves, they would eat the breakfast prepared for them by the Master, Yeshua.

John 21:12
> 12 Yeshua saith unto them, Come and dine. And none of the disciples durst ask him, Who art thou? knowing that it was the Lord. 13 Yeshua then cometh, and taketh bread, and giveth them, and fish likewise.

A SURFACE MEANING

Yeshua supplied these fishermen with an exceptional catch. This miracle identified to them, one more time, the risen Lord. We only need to look at the actions of Peter to see what excitement they had when they discovered this was Yeshua.

Yeshua, once again, provided for them, but their exceptional catch was incomparable to the source of that catch! Their Master, their friend and mentor, even though not physically accompanying them from place to place, still watched over them and knew their needs. He was with them!

A DEEPER MEANING

There is so much depth to this miracle. Through this miracle, the disciples gained greater faith, greater strength for their onward journey into the future, and here, Peter received lessons he would never forget. In the first catch of fish, Yeshua called Peter to be a fisher of men. Now, Peter's life would change again, but this time, his leadership of those men, and more importantly, his attitude in caring for them, Yeshua addressed.

John 21:12-17
> 12 Yeshua saith unto them, Come and dine. And none of the disciples durst ask him, Who art thou? knowing that it was the Lord. 13 Yeshua then cometh, and taketh bread, and giveth them, and fish likewise. 14 This is now the third time that Yeshua shewed himself to his disciples, after that he was risen from the dead.
>
> 15 ¶ So when they had dined, Yeshua saith to Simon Peter, Simon, son of Jonas, lovest thou me more than these? He saith unto him, Yea, Lord; thou knowest that I love thee. He saith unto him, Feed my lambs. 16 He saith to him again the second time, Simon, son of Jonas, lovest thou me? He saith unto him, Yea, Lord; thou knowest that I love thee. He saith unto him, Feed my sheep. 17 He saith unto him the third time, Simon, son of Jonas, lovest thou me? Peter was

grieved because he said unto him the third time, Lovest thou me? And he said unto him, Lord, thou knowest all things; thou knowest that I love thee. Yeshua saith unto him, Feed my sheep.

Yeshua, after taking care of their physical needs, satisfying their hunger, carried the lesson over to a very definite spiritual need. Yeshua knew many people who soon accepted Him as Saviour. They needed someone to care for them, as He cared for His disciples. Peter was one of those chosen vessels. As Peter cared for those sheep, however, it must be with deep love, and not just carry a surface interest. Peter must learn to care for God's sheep in the same manner, with the same heart as his Lord and Master.

Yes, Peter would love the Lord's sheep, and that love would take him to a place where one day, he'd die for his Lord. Of this Yeshua spoke next:

John 21:18-19

18 Verily, verily, I say unto thee, When thou wast young, thou girdedst thyself, and walkedst whither thou wouldest: but when thou shalt be old, thou shalt stretch forth thy hands, and another shall gird thee, and carry thee whither thou wouldest not. 19 This spake he, signifying by what death he should glorify God. And when he had spoken this, he saith unto him, Follow me.

It would cost Peter everything to serve Yeshua. The very depth of Peter's love would see Peter carried away to be crucified. In that death, he would bring God glory. In other words, Yeshua gave it all, and so would Peter! It will cost him to serve the Lord, to care for the Lord's sheep, and in the end, to suffer an agonizing death.

MINDSETS CHALLENGED

Encounters with Yeshua, throughout the Word of God, show people whose lives changed because of Yeshua's words, or actions in their life. When Yeshua walked the earth with His disciples, He ensured their needs were met, even supernaturally if need be. Now that Yeshua fully completed His mission as Saviour of the World, He would not physically be there, but they would need to know that He still watched over them, and if they could recall His Words from earlier, they would know that He would send them a Comforter.

John 16:7
> 7 Nevertheless I tell you the truth; It is expedient for you that I go away: for if I go not away, the Comforter will not come unto you; but if I depart, I will send him unto you.

Past that, to the immediate need at hand, Peter must know what lies within his own heart. This, Yeshua drew from Peter's innermost being, helping Peter to see that he indeed loved Yeshua, even above his own life. Earlier Peter denied that he knew Yeshua, and while Yeshua forgave that denial, the pain of that denial needed healing. Yeshua, with His dialogue with Peter, used words to heal the rift in Peter's heart and planted within Peter a firm conviction that renunciation would never happen again. No, Peter would not run in fear again! His life, empowered by the Holy One of Israel, shifted his life, changing it forever.

Later, while declaring the gospel against Rome's bann on it, they crucified Peter for his faith and expression of the gospel message. He indeed loved Yeshua enough to give his life for Him.

Reflection Time:

It is often very easy to speak about Yeshua when all the situations are favourable. Favourable circumstances, however, are not always possible, especially in cases where believers in Yeshua risk their life in sharing their faith. Take some time, alone with the Lord. Ask Him if your faith is deep, with a love for Him that no unfavourable circumstances can thwart or unearth from your heart.

CONCLUSION

Looking at the miracles over nature, we see:

WATER TURNED INTO WINE:
At a wedding, Yeshua provided a needed supply of wine and hence eliminated a humiliating embarrassment for the bride and groom. The platform of lack, within this miracle gave Yeshua much room to begin changing the mindset of His disciples. That mindset, shifting from the natural to the supernatural, from the human to the Divine was necessary if these disciples would bear the fruit Yeshua required of them. This new mindset, shifting focus to what God can do and forgetting mankind's limitations, proved itself essential for the disciples to grasp better Yeshua's overall mission upon the earth.

Cana's wedding, the platform on earth for His first public miracle, was not Yeshua's own wedding, but His day will come! First, His disciples and others receive Him as Saviour, and following that, they must also learn to embrace Him as the Bridegroom of Heaven, the betrothed of His beloved Bride upon the earth. As that bridegroom, He left this earth and went to His Father's House where He lives and prepares a place for His Bride. Then, at the time when the Father gives the go ahead, that trumpet sounds and Yeshua, in complete readiness, returns to this earth to take His Bride home with Him, forever.

Perhaps, on the day of the wedding at Cana, His disciples did not understand the comparison. Afterwards, when Yeshua had risen and opened their minds to the scriptures, they embraced this important concept, as well as the necessary mindset changes to see Him as God, and Lord of all!

CATCH OF A GREAT NUMBER OF FISH

Yeshua took Peter and his fishing partners out to Sea. Obedience to Yeshua's words resulted in a large catch of fish. So great was the weight of that catch, that the two ships, filled to the brim with the catch, sank lower in the water. From this miracle, Peter saw something in Yeshua that caused him to realize his own sinfulness. From that declaration of Peter, Yeshua extended a call to Peter to fish for "men" for God's Kingdom. As the platform for the miracle realized God's provision in an abundant manner, these disciples learned, first hand, God's supernatural ability to provide for them and their families. Thus, they were now free to follow Yeshua, to learn from Him and fully realize the depth of the divine call God entrusted to them. In future days, after Yeshua returned to Heaven, the catch of "men" would far exceed the catch of fish on that day. God, indeed, had greater purposes in mind for these fishermen. Praise the Lord, their mindsets shifted to embrace the call of God on their life!

STORMY SEA CALMED

Amidst a stormy sea, in a tiny sailing vessel, Yeshua slept. Aroused by His disciples, who felt all would drown in the sea, Yeshua rebuked the wind and the waves. "Who is this mankind that even nature obeys His Voice?" He is none other than the son of God, the Holy One of Israel. He is God incarnate, standing in their midst.

This platform for a miracle saw the realization of physical salvation from the raging sea for all within the tiny ship. Soon, at a time in the future, Yeshua would not be found physically sleeping in the hinder part of the ship, but He rests, sitting at the right Hand of His Father, on high. His disciples must understand that His place of rest shifted from the tiny ship to His eternal place in the heavens. Nevertheless, He is still with them, just as real, just as concerned about their welfare, and even more powerful than those days in the ship, tossed by a raging sea. They can count on that!

Later, as they looked back on that miracle, they had a history lesson in real life, showing them that nothing, not even the forces of nature, extend beyond the control of their Saviour and Lord! This they learned, also, through other lessons and miracles, where Yeshua exercised power over the elements of this earth, including His Resurrection, for Yeshua's powers surpassed death and the grave!

FEEDING THE MULTITUDE

Sitting in a desert place with five thousand men, plus women and children, (and another time with 4,000 men plus women and children,) the disciples witnessed Yeshua as the Master of even the supernatural. How great was Yeshua's faith! How mighty was God's provision through Him! How amazing to walk with the One who provides for all needs, no matter the number, no matter the situation! How awesome is this Yeshua, Who taught them to look past their physical needs to see Him as the bread of life! All they must do is believe! Yes, they must raise their eyes past the circumstances of this earth, upward, to God's planned agenda for their life: *the provision of the Son of God for their eternal wellbeing in all things.*

MONEY IN FISH'S MOUTH

As Yeshua sent Peter to catch a fish with a coin in its mouth, to pay the temple tax, we see the Kingship of Yeshua, for He, the Son of God, need pay no temple tax at all. Only God could produce a miracle like this one, calling a fish to hold a coin in its mouth; sending Peter into the vast sea, and placing that fish where it would be caught! There is no limit to God's ability to provide, and even the creativity of His provision. Surely, Peter can trust in the ability of God to provide, especially considering Yeshua later commanded him to feed His sheep!

FIG TREE WITHERS

Walking from Bethany to Jerusalem, we see a fig tree withered because it bore no fruit from which Yeshua could eat! This fig tree was symbolic, but of what? It displayed the doctrines and teachings of the scholars of Israel, the ones who were given the care of the sheep of the Almighty. With their manmade conclusions and darkened eyes, they robbed fruit from the tree of life. Yeshua cursed that fig tree, so it would never bear fruit again. How God hates the doctrines and teachings of men! It is the scriptures that spoke of Yeshua! In that light, perceive them! In that light receive them! Let all other teachings, let all other Messiahs, fade away, wither, and die like the fig tree! May all eyes focus on the One Who is the Way, the Truth, and the Life!

WALKING ON WATER

As Yeshua walked upon water, His Disciples saw, yet again, His ability to overcome the sea and wind. Rightly they concluded, Yeshua is the Son of the

Living God. This truth, they needed embed into the depth of their being. It must embed in us also! Yeshua's life, death, burial, resurrection, ascension, and position at God's right Hand are basic doctrinal stones of our foundation! It cemented powerful disciples in the early church, and it does the same today!

SECOND CATCH OF FISH

This second catch of fish took place after the Resurrection. After the catch was realized, Peter swam briskly to shore to meet Yeshua, the Master, Who, once more, was with them! In that meeting, Yeshua healed the rift in Peter's heart after he denied the Messiah three times. Also, Yeshua brought forth Peter's love for Him, commanding Him to care for the sheep of His kingdom. Peter's love was enough and yes, strong enough to follow Yeshua to the cross. Peter indeed would follow Yeshua's words, "Come Follow Me".

SUMMARY OF WORKS ABOVE NATURE:

With each miracle above nature, Yeshua turned to His Heavenly Father, and with His faith and trust in Him, saw the power of the Holy Spirit bring forth the miracles into existence. He rested in His relationship with the Father, and in His good will for all humankind. As we look at the miracles in this section, we see but a few, yet they are ample to show God's seal upon His Son, Yeshua! They stand, also, as an example to all believers that with God, all things are possible!

Like all scripture, studying it compares to digging for gold, as layer after layer brings amazing treasures. Every treasure in these miracles, every lesson learned, one person could not possibly write in one book. So, dear reader, keep what you've learned.

In our closing reflection, let's remember the words of Nicodemus:

> John 3:1-2
> 1 ¶ There was a mankind of the Pharisees, named Nicodemus, a ruler of the Jews: 2 The same came to Yeshua by night, and said unto him, Rabbi, we know that thou art a teacher come from God: for no mankind can do these miracles that thou doest, except God be with him.

To know Yeshua came from God is important, but there is another important lesson that many, unfortunately, overlook and it is this:

to take every situation in your life and turn it into a platform for a miracle.

If the situation is desperate, it makes a good platform or springboard for the Lord to arrive and show Himself as God. If the situation is a pleasant one, it is also a good place for God to receive glory for His blessings, and of course, if the situation is sort of mundane, it is also a place for God to show Himself strong, for He breathes life into every place He enters.

So, dear reader, remember, the secret to seeing God's Hand manifest in your life is not really a secret, at all is it? No, it is the ability of the believer to take every situation in their life and turn it over to the touch of the living God, remembering that "The eyes of the Lord look to and fro through all the earth for a place to show Himself strong".

As you ponder on your life and your relationship with the Almighty, give every place in your life to the Lord, no matter if it seems to be a good place, a mundane place or one somewhere in between. Then, when a difficult place arises, you will be ready to take that place before the Lord as a platform for a miracle and be confident that He will show Himself strong!

In closing this book, tuck yourself beneath the wings of the Almighty. Thank Him that in every challenging situation, He is there with you, and you are, *and always will be,* a Candidate for a Miracle!

APPENDIX

A Name to Honour

YeHoVaH[93]

If, today, someone asked you to tell them the name of your earthly father, without hesitation you would declare it. If, for some reason, you did not know the identity of your earthly father, you would say so. You might even give an explanation as to why that might be so. Thus said, if asked to relate the name of your heavenly Father, today, would you do so with ease, or would you draw a blank?

Most of Christendom, today, is ignorant *as to the name of the Father*, as well as the way to pronounce it. As the author of this book, I would like to join the ranks of those who wish to relate that name to the world. I believe that when we stand before the Father on the day that we give an account for our deeds in this body, it would be a good thing to know His Son, His Name!

About The Name

---

[93] Based on information given by Michael Rood. Some from his work entitled, The Chronological Bible, and some from his YouTube videos. For more information see page 28 of the Chronological Bible.

Did you know that the name of the Father appears at least 6,828 times in the Hebrew scriptures? Scribes recorded it with four specific Hebrew letters. They are as follows:

י	Pronounced yode, or yod
ה	Pronounced as hey
ו	Pronounced as Vav
ה	Pronounced as hey

For centuries, whenever the Jews come across these 4 letters they simply say, Adonai, or Ha Shem (meaning the name). They refuse to pronounce the name for several reasons, some of which we will look at momentarily. For now, let us look at whether their tradition affected Christianity. That we can easily do by looking at our Bibles to see the 4-letter name of the Father either written or substituted.

A quick look reveals that our KVJ Bibles, as well as many other versions, the 4-letter name presented to readers is a 4-letter English word, "LORD" [94]. Whether intentional or not, Christendom has followed the ancient tradition of the Jews.

An Ancient Tradition

In early second century times[95] Rabbis hid the pronunciation of the holy name of God. They did this

---

[94] In some translations it is GOD.
[95] Some scholars even dating further back.

by omitting the vowel pointings, which are necessary to make the name pronounceable. Hence, as they carefully wrote the scriptures, their omittance of the vowel pointings made the name unpronounceable. Historians believe there were two reasons why they did this:

i. According to Josephus, Rome, under the rule of Domitian, 81 to 96 CE, put to death anyone using the name of the Jewish or Christian God.
ii. Many believe that the Rabbis borrowed a tradition from pagans, whereby the name of their god was considered too holy to mention, so they called him "Ba-al" meaning Lord. The Jews adopted this practice and most still practice it today, even some Messianic Jews!

Tradition Continues

Bible translators followed their tradition for many reasons which are not presently known. It is possible, they forgot the pronunciation of the name, but more than likely, those who knew it, hid it.[96] Whatever the reason, following this tradition caused Christians to continue in this tradition.

Does that tradition offend
the Heavenly Father?

---

[96] According to some, the Jews secretly knew the name.

If indeed its origin was Baal worship, then we can give a resounding Amen to the fact it offends God. In addition, as we look at scripture, we see the Almighty was not pleased with this, for His Heart desires all to enjoy salvation, including the Gentiles. How can that happen if they do not know upon what name they should call? Scripture [97] clearly says in the end times, Gentiles will know His name and call upon it to receive salvation. Obviously, for that to happen, they must know the name of YeHoVaH (יְהֹוָה).

An Historic Discovery

Today, some Hebrew scholars[98] have searched the world over for Hebrew manuscripts. In doing so, they found many Hebrew documents have the full name with vowels and therefore the pronunciation of the name. These scholars may different slightly in pronunciation, but nevertheless, they are making the name of YeHoVaH known today.

Our Saviour's Name Hidden in This Name

In looking at the Hebrew root of the name of the Father, pronounced *Yah-Ho **Vah'***, and looking at another scripture, we see something amazing about

---

[97] Jeremiah 16:1-21
[98] Nehemiah Gordon, a Hebrew scholar, according to his testimony, found the name of the Father with all vowel pointings in the Aleppo Codex, and through his efforts, and those of others discovered that name with vowel pointings in over 2000 manuscripts.

our Saviour. In speaking of the Prophet, the one the Father would send and to whom all must listen and obey, YeHoVaH said that His name would be in the name of the Prophet.

Exodus 23:21 "Beware of him, and obey his voice, provoke him not; for he will not pardon your transgressions[99]: *for my name [is] in him*".

Our Saviour's name, as given by the angel was "Yehoshua", which means Salvation.

That name, with its Hebrew letters reads as:

י	**Pronounced yode or yod**
ה	**Pronounced hey**
ו	**Pronounced vav**
שׁ	Pronounced shin
ע	Pronounced ayin

The name of the Father (יְהֹוָה) is in the name of the Son! The first three letters of YeHoVaH show it! (Yod, Heh, Vav). Is it so amazing that the name of our Father is in the true name of the One YeHoVaH sent to redeem us!

---

[99] Please keep in mind that Yeshua bore the punishment for your sins. Your sins were not pardoned, they were atoned!

Honour the Father's Name

Throughout this book, and all later books, as well as all accompanying audios and PowerPoints, it is the author's intention to widely use, proclaim and continually pronounce the name of the Father, as well as the name of Yeshua. Indeed, this breaks with tradition of many, however, thus far as we have shared the news of the Father's name and use Yeshua's birth name, reception has been excellent.

Name Challenge

Since, as of this reading, you are no longer ignorant of your heavenly Father's name, we invite you to join the unofficial network of proclaimers of the Father's name and shout it from the house tops. In doing so, you honour the Heavenly Father, our Savour Yeshua, and the Holy Spirit.

> Romans 10:12-15
> *"12   For there is no difference between the Jew and the Greek: for the same Lord over all is rich unto all that call upon him. 13 For whosoever shall call upon the name of the Lord shall be saved. 14 How then shall they call on him in whom they have not believed? and how shall they believe in him of whom they have not heard? and how shall they hear without a preacher? 15 And how shall they preach, except they be sent? as it is written, How beautiful are the feet of them that preach the gospel of peace and bring glad tidings of good things!"*

ABOUT THE KING JAMES VERSION

Scriptures quoted in this book *originate* from the KJV **public domain version** of the Bible, which means, no copyright exists on this version of the scripture. While some find this translation outdated, Jeanne, trained in the KJV still finds this version helpful, and uses it in all her books[100].

In using KJV, however, it is good to remember the following:

- Some words in the KJV have changed meaning over the centuries. To understand such words, look up the root word in its original language. In doing so, the meaning stands out. For example. KJV uses the word "conversation" however, in its original language it means moral character, or behaviour.
- When KJV spoke of humanity, they said, "mankind". When you read that word, or hear others speak about the scriptures using the term, "mankind", know it refers to all humankind, not a specific gender.

Due to tradition, the name of the Father, YeHoVaH appears as LORD, or at times as Jehovah. However, in all Jeanne's manuscripts, YeHoVaH's name replaces the term LORD. "A Name to Honour", located in the Appendix section explains it further.

---

[100] In later manuscripts, the author updated the more archaic words in the KJV such as wouldest or couldest.

SALVATION'S MESSAGE

Yeshua, when walking on earth, said this:
> *John 3:14-18*
> *14 And as Moses lifted up the serpent in the wilderness, even so must the Son of mankind be lifted up: 15 That whosoever believes in him should not perish but have eternal life. 16 For God so loved the world, that he gave his only begotten Son, that whosoever believes in him should not perish, but have everlasting life. 17 For God sent not his Son into the world to condemn the world; but that the world through him might be saved. 18 He that believes on him is not condemned: but he that believes not is condemned already, because he hath not believed in the name of the only begotten Son of God.*

During the time of Moses, the children of Israel, in the wilderness, rebelled against God, at which time poisonous serpents infiltrated the camp, killing many of the people. After seeking YeHoVaH for a solution to the problem, Moses followed God's instructions and made a bronze serpent fashioned and erected it on a pole in sight of the people. Whosoever wanted to live, must acknowledge their rebellion against YeHoVaH, and in doing so, look upon the erected pole and bronze serpent, to YeHoVaH, who gave them life in place of death, then they would live.

Yeshua said, just as Moses erected that bronze serpent in the wilderness, He would be lifted up. This referred to the event, in the future, of Yeshua's crucifixion. During the time when the serpent hung on that pole, whosoever wanted to live and not die from the serpent's bite must acknowledge their rebellion, their sin against YeHoVaH.

Likewise, for those who wish to live eternally, they must look upon the cross of the crucified One, to YeHoVaH, who provided life for them. This was an act of love for all humankind, necessary because mankind is born from Adam, and thus is born with an inherent sin.

Secondly, mankind sins. The consequence of sin is death, and eternal death, wherein mankind will spend an eternity in darkness, away from YeHoVaH. Unfortunately, there is nothing humanly possible to reverse those consequences. Even if a person had made a genuine decision never to sin again, and for some reason they succeeded, all their virtuous deeds and good living would not erase the penalty of eternal death.

There is only *one way* for Eternal Life to touch a person's life. That way Yeshua explained to His listeners as *through the cross.*

Salvation comes by understanding these facts:
1. Yeshua, being the Son of God and the fulfilment of the scriptures, never sinned.

2. YeHoVaH, on behalf of every human being on the earth, chose to make Yeshua become as sin, in His Eyes, so that Yeshua might pay the penalty for sin, for all of humanity.
3. Yeshua paid that penalty. He died on the cross and was buried in a tomb.
4. Three days later, He rose again, appearing to His disciples, to show them the reality of His resurrection, to show them God vindicated Him and made Him both Lord and Messiah.
5. Yeshua could not stay in the tomb, because "death" comes to all who sin, but since Yeshua never sinned, therefore, death could not hold Him in the grave.
6. All those who come to Yeshua, to receive Him as their Saviour, receive liberty from sin and from its horrible consequence, eternal death.
7. They enter YeHoVaH's Kingdom and receive eternal life, as well as another gift: **The Righteousness of Messiah.** After salvation, when YeHoVaH looks upon a believer in Messiah, He sees Yeshua's perfect life and sees a redeemed believer, set aside for YeHoVaH. Since salvation has taken place in the believer, the Holy Spirit dwells within them.
8. All it takes to receive salvation from YeHoVaH is receiving His Messiah, fully repenting from

sinning against God[101]. YeHoVaH even gives the believer the faith to receive His gift of Salvation!

The Apostle Paul put it this way:
Ephesians 2:8
"For by grace are ye saved through faith; and that not of yourselves: it is the gift of God"

When you pray the following prayer, realize we present it here to get you started in your walk with YeHoVaH. Living out your salvation depends upon your commitment to follow through *from this point onward*. From the moment of your commitment and onward, dear one, please seek YeHoVaH for His help in all things, including help to make your life align with truth, and in the end be a praise unto His name, forever!

---

[101] And against mankind. When a person steals, etc. they sin against both God and mankind. PLEASE NOTE: all references to "mankind", either by scripture or the author, refers to all humankind, not a specific gender.

SINNER'S PRAYER & LIFETIME COMMITMENT

Heavenly, Father:

I acknowledge before You, Lord, that I am a sinner. I understand sin's punishment is a life without You, for all eternity. Thank You for sending Yeshua to the earth, as the Messiah. I understand now that He died in my place, to take my punishment for my sins. I believe You raised Yeshua from the dead, and now that I accepted Him as my personal Saviour, my old life dies, and my new life begins.

I humbly ask You, Lord, to forgive me of my sins, and as of this moment, I receive Yeshua as my Mashiach. I open my heart to receive the works of the cross that You provided for me through Yeshua, and with Your help, I will walk away from my sin, turning my back upon my own will and ways. I will now live my life seeking to obey Your Word and Your will. Help me to live, from this point onward, in a manner pleasing to You.

One more thing:

Remember, this gospel message comes with power. When you hear it, the Kingdom of God draws near to you. When you repent of your sins and receive salvation, the Kingdom of God moves within. You cannot see it, feel it, or tell it from an outward observance. It is accepted, received, and lived out by faith! Seek out other believers in Messiah and may God bless you richly as you live your live, now, completely for Him!

So now, be sure and tell someone!
Remember that a person believes with the heart unto righteousness and confesses with their mouth unto salvation, as spoken about in *Romans 10:10, which says, "For with the heart mankind believes unto righteousness; and with the mouth confession is made unto salvation"*.

SCRIPTURE INDEX

1

1 Corinthians 11:24-26 99
1 Corinthians 2:16..... 32
1 Corinthians 2:9....... 43
1 John 1:7 99
1 John 4: 9 93
1 Peter 2:24 40

2

2 Chronicles 16:9....... 56
2 Chronicles 16:9 a) .. 17
2 Corinthians 1:20..... 51
2 Kings 4:1-7.............. 89
2 Kings 5:11-15........ 115

A

Acts 10: 34-35.............. 74
Acts 2:36................... 206

C

Colossians 1:12-13 .. 203

D

Daniel 11:32 b........... 252
Deuteronomy 6:4.... 206

E

Ephesians 2:8........... 241
Exodus 23:21 235

G

Galatians 3:11.......... 150
Galatians 3:24.......... 188
Galatians 4:22-31 186
Genesis 18:14 9
Genesis 3:7............... 182

H

Habakkuk 2:4.......... 150
Hebrews 10:14......... 190
Hebrews 10:38......... 196
Hebrews 10:38:........ 150
Hebrews 11:6..... 48, 204
Hebrews 13:5........... 152
Hebrews 13:8............ 42
Hebrews 7:25............ 22
Hebrews 9:13-14 100
Hebrews 9:14........... 204

I

Isaiah 25:1 162
Isaiah 42:1 124
Isaiah 46:10 29

Isaiah 52:13 124
Isaiah 55:10 141
Isaiah 55:9 31
Isaiah 61:1-2................ 24
Isaiah 61:1-3.................. 4

J

Jeremiah 16:1-2 234
Jeremiah 32: 27........ 126
Jeremiah 8:11-13 183
John
  2:1-11 82
John 1:10-14 202
John 1:14 .... 140, 205
John 1:36 82
John 10:10 25
John 10:9 46
John 12:31 36
John 12:6 171
John 14:12-13 24
John 14:2 94
John 14:6 47
John 15: 3 97
John 16: 11 36
John 16:13 189
John 16:7 217
John 16:8-11 36
John 19:26-27 125
John 2:11 97
John 2:4b 92

John 2:5 87
John 21:1-11 210
John 21:12 214
John 21:12-17 215
John 21:18-19 216
John 3:1-2 225
John 3:15-16 50
John 6: 21 198
John 6:14-15 160
John 6:26-27 161
John 6:28 162
John 6:29 163
John 6:30 163
John 6:32-40 163
John 6:63 148
John 7:38-39 98

L

Luke 5
  1-11 110
Luke 5: 8-9 114
Luke 5:10................... 114
Luke 5:11................... 116
Luke 6:38................... 118

M

Malachi 3:6 41
Mark 11:12-14.......... 180
Mark 14:35b............... 92
Mark 4

35-41 129
Mark 4: 35 b 141
Mark 4: 41 136
Mark 4:39 b 131
Mark 4:40 138
Mark 4:41 132
Mark 6
  35-44 156
Mark 6:30-34 156
Mark 6:37 157
Mark 6:45-52 198
Matthew 14:31 203
Matthew 17
  24-27 169
Matthew 17:25 b to 26
  170
Matthew 21
  18-22 179
Matthew 21:14-16 ... 185
Matthew 21:21 181
Matthew 21:22 190
Matthew 28:20 b 143
Matthew 4:19 174
Matthew 5:18 184
Matthew 8:14 125
Matthew 8:16-17 39

P

Philippians 4:11 123
Proverbs 3: 5 139
Proverbs 4:20-22 148
Psalm 103:1-5 22
Psalm 115:11 139
Psalm 119:89 15
Psalm 12: 6 149
Psalm 139:11-13 138
Psalm 139:1-6 177
Psalm 18:6 45
Psalm 32:8-9 119
Psalm 46: 1-3 144
Psalm 46:1 151

R

Revelation 13:8 33
Romans 1:17 150
Romans 10:12-15 236
Romans 11:1, 5-8 193

Z

Zephaniah 3:17 134

MIRACLE SUBDIVISION INDEX

Background Setting

CHAPTER #	5	6	7	8	9	10	11	12
PAGE #	85	110	130	156	170	180	199	210

Operative Mindsets

CHAPTER #	5	6	7	8	9	10	11	12
PAGE #	86	112	130	157	171	181	199	211

Miracle Platform

CHAPTER #	5	6	7	8	9	10	11	12
PAGE #	86	113	131	158	171	187	200	212

Revelation of God

CHAPTER #	5	6	7	8	9	10	11	12
PAGE #	88	114	132	158	172	189	201	212

Miracle Specifics

CHAPTER #	5	6	7	8	9	10	11	12
PAGE #	92	115	135	159	173	190	202	204

A Surface Meaning

CHAPTER #	5	6	7	8	9	10	11	12
PAGE #	95	116	137	159	173	192	203	214

A Deeper Meaning

CHAPTER #	5	6	7	8	9	10	11	12
PAGE #	96	118	140	161	174	192	204	215

Mindsets Challenged								
CHAPTER #	5	6	7	8	9	10	11	12
PAGE #	100	121	144	165	174	195	205	217

REFLECTION INDEX

1st Large Catch of Fish.............................	105
2nd Catch of Fish	123
Feeding of the 5,000	151
Fig Tree Withers.......................................	165
Money in Fish's Mouth...........................	176
Stormy Sea Calmed.................................	196
Walking on the Water.............................	207
Water Turned into Wine.........................	218
Conclusion...	225

OTHER BOOKS BY THIS AUTHOR

Jeanne writes mostly Bible Studies which are also good reading. Each study comes with a textbook and workbook. Unless otherwise specified in the footnote, consider this a list of available Bible Studies.

An Arsenal of Powerful Prayers [102]
   Scriptural Prayers to Move Mountains,
Arising Incense
   A Believer's Priesthood
Candidate for A Miracle
   Wisdom from the miracles of Yeshua
Foundations of Revival
   Biblical Evidence for Revival
His Reflection
   What God longs to see in His People
Heaven's Greater Government
   Behind the Scenes of Earth's Events
In The Name of Yehovah We Set Up Our Banners
   Biblical use of banners
It's All About Heaven
   As Pictured in Scripture
Kingdom Keys for Kingdom Kids
   Walking in Kingdom Power
Molded for the Miraculous
   Why God made You

---

[102] This is a book of written prayers of assorted topics to help believers live a stronger, active faith. No workbook.

Releasing the Impossible (Volumes)
  The Limitless Power of Intercession
  Volume 1: Intercessions from the Author's Life
  Volume 2: Intercessions from Biblical Characters
Salvation Depicted in a Meal [103]
  Passover Hagaddah
The Jeremiah Generation
  God's Response to Injustice
The Warrior Bride-
  God's Kingdom Advancing through Spiritual Warfare
Thy Kingdom Come
  Entering God's Rest in Prayer
Watching, Waiting, Warning
  Obeying Yeshua's Command to Watch & Pray
When Nations Rumble
  A Study of the Book of Amos
Worship in Spirit and In Truth [104]
  The Tabernacle of David - Past, Present & Future

To keep updated on what is available, please check our website for all manuscripts in print and/or check on Amazon for books obtained through their website in 16 countries.

www.cegullahpublishing.ca

---

[103] Haggadah (Guide) for a Christian Passover. No Workbook.
[104] Good sister book to "In the Name of YeHoVaH we set up our banners".

ABOUT JEANNE METCALF

Jeanne believes the Word of God opens a door to help every believer to know their God. That knowledge, once gleaned and retained, makes strong believers to help them stand in the real world in which we live, no matter their vocation.

With these convictions in mind, Jeanne, inspired and led by the Holy Spirit, began to write in the 1990's. Soon she developed inductive[105] style Bible Studies and self-published them for her students to use. With her major goal to equip the saints, she found that her sound teachings, presented with clarity and simplicity, made an impact. As long as her listeners put in their valuable time to study scripture and took Jeanne's advice to call upon the Holy Spirit to help them, they became powerful believers, transformed, prepared and ready to stand in their generation.

Today, past students who studied the Bible with Jeanne, as well current new students, testify as to the

---

[105] In the inductive Bible Study method, believers learn first by reading and studying the Word on their own, then they glean from the textbook. This study method often gives a better foundation to a believer's faith than sitting through lectures or speaker related teachings.

validity of Jeanne's writing and teaching gift. They love the clarity and simplicity of the Word as she presents it in a refreshing straightforward format. Thus, they encouraged Jeanne to make her books more widely available.

Therefore, Jeanne began Cegullah Publishing, and then a year later, opened Cegullah Apologetic Academy. The academy, in addition to presenting accredited, Bible Study material, invites all believers to read or study the Word of God, and thereby, be strong in YeHoVaH and the strength of His might.

A greater availability of Jeanne's works (as well as other authors which Cegullah Publishing looks forward to publishing in the future), opens doors for more people to know their God and do exploits!

"But the people that know their God shall be strong and do exploits". Daniel 11:32 b

***

About CP & AA
CEGULLAH PUBLISHING & APOLOGETICS ACADEMY.

We publish books as well as teach accredited and unaccredited courses. Since our book content is based upon the Bible, the Word of God, we consider our books as treasures. Through these available treasures, we give opportunities for our readers and students to explore pertinent topics which steady, reaffirm, and help them to walk out their life in victory.

Our Vision
- To supply Christian, Bible-based materials to help readers study God's Word

Our Focus
- To help our readers to know *what they believe and why.*

Our Mission
- To provide bible studies, devotionals, teachings, and other educational tools to help readers to know their God and connect with Him.

Our Publishing Motto:
- *Publishing the treasures of modern-day scribes.*

Our Academy Motto:
- *Earnestly contend for the faith once given to the saints.*

CONTACT INFORMATION
www.cegullahpublishing.ca

www.ingramcontent.com/pod-product-compliance
Lightning Source LLC
Chambersburg PA
CBHW071153160426
43196CB00011B/2065